Victory in JESUS

Embracing His Death and Receiving His Overcoming Life

Bill Liversidge

CREATIVE GROWTH MINISTRIES
PALM SPRINGS, CALIFORNIA

Editing and page composition by Ken McFarland
Copy editing and proofreading by Ann Anderson
Cover art direction and design by Ed Guthero
Cover illustration by Robert Grace

Copyright © 2007 by Bill Liversidge
Printed in the United States of America
All Rights Reserved

Unless otherwise indicated, Scripture references are from the New American Standard Bible®, copyright © 1960, 1962, 1963, 1968, 1971, 1972, 1973, 1975, 1977, 1995 by The Lockman Foundation. Used by permission.

Scriptures from the New King James Version are copyrighted © 1982 by Thomas Nelson, Inc. Used by permission. All rights reserved.

ISBN: 978-0-9793409-0-1
ISBN: 0-9793409-0-X

Contents

Foreword iv
Acknowledgments vi
Dedication vii
About the Author viii
1 Grace—the Real and the Counterfeit 11
2 Two Views of Salvation 17
3 The Line Between Faith and Works 23
4 Means—or Fruit? 27
5 The Source of Our Peace 33
6 Salvation—Accomplished Fact and Ongoing Process 39
7 The Truth That Shakes the World 43
8 Adventists and Righteousness By Faith 49
9 "Having Been…We Shall Be" 53
10 The Most Important Daily Habit 63
11 Faith Statements 69
12 What a Relief It Is! 77
13 "Much More" 87
14 Baptism, Death, and Life 93
15 Joining the Body of Christ 101
16 A Radical Inner Change 105
17 The Mind of Christ 115
18 New Spiritual Habits 129
19 All That You Need Is in Jesus 135
20 Victory Through Surrender 141
21 Carnal—or Spiritual? 151
22 The Old—and the New 159
Appendix 165

Foreword

Are you struggling with temptation and sin? Are there things in your life that it seems Christ has been unable to overcome? Are you wondering if victory will ever happen? Are you getting discouraged, beginning to think that you are a lost cause? Is your faith at a low ebb? Perhaps you've even come to the point where you've started to believe that you might as well enjoy the sin if you are going to be stuck with it!

Or maybe you just don't feel that you are measuring up to the high standard of God's character. The "fruit of the Spirit"—love, joy, peace, patience, kindness, goodness, faithfulness, gentleness, and self-control (Galatians 5:22-23)—is not being consistently revealed in your life.

Please know that you are not alone. Many Christians, including myself, have had this same experience. We all continue to have a need to live by faith in the overcoming Christ and in His love for us—to walk in the sure knowledge in our hearts and minds that He loves us with an unconditional love—that He is able, willing and faithful to overcome the sin and character defects in our lives by living in us through the Holy Spirit!

What you are about to read is the result of *Victory in Jesus* seminars given by Pastor Bill Liversidge in various locations around the world. I have been privileged to attend a number of these seminars and have been immeasurably blessed every time by the Good News so clearly presented.

Victory in Jesus is based on the book of Romans, chapters 5 through 8. In this book Pastor Bill Liversidge, speaker/director of Creative Growth Ministries, will lead you into a clear understanding of the Good News. The death of Jesus is the essential foundation to understanding and receiving all that God desires for you. You will know the truth of salvation, victory, and righteousness through the death and indwelling life of Christ, who is the solution for the sin problem. You will gain in these pages not only a theological knowledge of Christian victory but also practical steps to put into place that will yield powerful changes in your life. You will no longer find yourself needing to ask forgiveness for the same old sins over and over again. Pastor Bill presents some very Good News indeed.

I pray that this practical guide to victory will strengthen you, that you will be revived in your walk with Christ, that you will once again be restored to a faith which believes that with Christ all things are possible, and that you will experience true, lasting freedom through an ever-deepening relationship with Him.

"For I am not ashamed of the gospel, for it is the power of God for salvation to everyone who believes, to the Jew first and also to the Greek. For in it the righteousness of God is revealed from faith to faith; as it is written, *'but the righteous* man *shall live by faith'*" Romans 1:16, 17 (emphasis added).

Ann Anderson

Acknowledgments

Special thanks are due...

...to the many participants in seminars, whose patience and diligent digging in the Word enabled me to clarify the issues resonating in *Victory in Jesus*.

...to Ken McFarland, an editor of exceptional skill, who took seminar transcripts and turned them into a dynamic book.

...to Ann Anderson, whose untiring efforts and superb theological insights enabled me to keep the Good News crystal clear and to bring this project to completion.

And special praise to God for His generosity in trusting such sublime themes to one who is so undeserving.

Dedication

To Dorothy Liversidge, my mother,
whose faith propelled me into ministry.

Bill Liversidge

INDUCTIVE TEACHER OF THE WORD

Bill Liversidge is a native of Melbourne, Australia. His forty-year ministry has included ten years as a missionary in New Guinea, church pastoring, college teaching, as well as department leadership at the union conference level.

He attended Avondale College in Australia, Andrews University Theological Seminary in Berrien Springs Michigan, and Fuller Theological Seminary in Pasadena, California.

Pastor Liversidge has a highly developed teaching style based on the Inductive Method. The Inductive approach has led thousands of people to gain tremendous spiritual insights, conviction, and growth, since it can overcome preconceived notions and limited perspectives. The real power is in the Word, under the twin guidance provided by the Spirit and the Body.

Bill's students are highly motivated as they discover in group- and self-study the great truths of scripture. Profound discoveries have been made in the Word of God, and the book of Revelation especially has begun to yield its secrets through the group discovery process. Many have experienced life-changing encounters with God through dynamic seminars open to people of all faiths and denominations.

Bill's commitment to the "Priesthood of All Believers" and the biblical blueprint for church growth remains undiminished. As President for the past twenty years of Creative Growth Ministries—a supporting ministry of the Seventh-day Adventist Church—Pastor Liversidge is dedicated to equipping believers in the biblical principles they need to develop their spiritual gifts and move into effective ministry, revealing Christ and His character through His living Body—the Church. All members are thereby lifted up to their maximum God-intended potential within the whole Body.

CHAPTER ONE

Grace...the Real and the Counterfeit

Before you read this chapter, I want to urge you first to read Romans chapter 5 in your Bible. Go ahead and do that now—this book will still be here when you're done!

. . . OK, now let's consider a little background history, because I think we should be intelligent regarding the origins of our own movement. The fact that there is confusion at times among Protestants—especially on serious matters such as salvation—is undoubtedly a reflection of the fact that they have an insufficient knowledge of where and how the Protestant movement began.

Of course, to trace these beginnings, we need to go back to the Reformation. Protestants of all faiths have always been proud, in fact, of being able to say that they stand on the shoulders of the reformers.

The sixteenth century—when the Reformation began—followed after more than a thousand years, during which the religious world and even much of the political world was dominated by Roman Catholicism. According to Bible prophecy, this long era of the Dark Ages lasted for 1260 years. Through these centuries, Catholicism involved itself heavily in politics and attempted to control people's lives—even their individual relationships with God.

Throughout these Dark Ages, the Church forbade the common people access to the Bible. The priests became a controlling influence in people's lives. They had to trust the priest to tell them what God was like, how to relate to Him, and how He felt about them.

The Church even did its best to control people's means. They demanded the payment of fees called indulgences to purchase God's favor following their death—basically, prepaying the "wages" of sin. Martin Luther was especially offended by this concept of indulgences.

I think it's quite miraculous that God used a Catholic monk to launch the Reformation—it convinces me more strongly than ever that God is no respecter of persons. It doesn't matter what denomination is yours—or what religious convictions you have. If your heart is open toward God, you will be drawn to Him, and He will open to your mind an understanding of the truth about Himself.

We all know that God has precious children in every church. So we ought not to be surprised that in the darkest period of history in this world, God had precious children—even, incredibly, priests—whose hearts were actually open to hearing the truth about God, despite the fact that they were part of a system that was leading people astray. I think that's miraculous! It shows how gracious God is!

I'm a great admirer of Martin Luther. I know he was a rough, some might even say crude, man—but I like his strength of character. I like that when he came to a discovery biblically, he was courageous enough to stand firmly for it, even if all the winds were blowing against him. When ultimately, Martin Luther came before the Diet of Worms, all the bishops of Catholicism were there, and all the kings and emperors of Europe. Yet here's this humble, married monk, who fearlessly and firmly says to them all, "Here I stand, I can do no other—because it is written, 'The just shall live by faith.'" (See Romans 1:17.)

The Dark Ages—a thousand years, plus.

Why the "dark" ages?

No light. No light at all.

No light concerning what? Concerning—especially—what teaching?

The character of God.

And what particular aspect of God's character?

Grace.

God has always been so gracious to the human race. And Catholicism for centuries kept a wall of darkness between God's grace and the people He had created. The longer the Church reigned, the more dense grew the darkness. The Church twisted the definition of grace: it could be purchased—it could be earned.

People were taught that they could actually pay enough that God would feel just enough better toward them that He would reduce the thousands of years they would have to spend in purgatory. The few fortunate wealthy could pay their way right out of purgatory and go immediately, at death, to a higher place.

Yet today, some good Catholic people can be found in small Bible study groups in which they rediscover what Martin Luther found five hundred years ago—the Bible evidence for how gracious God is.

The Twelve Stations

The Catholic Church is known for its sacraments: confession, baptism, communion, the stations of the cross. In a Catholic Church you'll see magnificent pictures of Jesus en route to Calvary. The pictures portray twelve steps—the twelve stations—where believers can kneel before each one and recite a given number of rosaries.

The sacraments were designed by the Church to enable grace to come upon its members. In other words, if you observed the twelve stations of the cross and said "so many" rosaries, you'd get "this much" forgiveness.

But what should really occupy the place of the sacraments? There is really only one source of grace—and that Source is Jesus! There is only one Mediator between God and man—"the man Christ Jesus" 1 Timothy 2:5. "There is no other name...given among men by which we must be saved"—except Jesus Christ. Acts 4:12.

You see, Christians in the Protestant tradition believe that Jesus has opened the door for the grace of God to come upon people freely. But the Catholic system—and it's important to grasp this—has always been a system where people do things that they hope will enable God to feel better toward them. It was—and is—a system based on human works.

The chances of receiving light, for those born into Catholicism, are limited, because systems tend to perpetuate themselves. Some Protestants have their own struggles in this area, let's face it. I don't mind telling you that if you really preached free grace today, you could be stoned or in some places. I'm serious—even in supposedly Christian churches.

Someone sitting out there listening to the good news of free grace may say, "Oh, thank You, God! I feel hope for the first time! For the first time in my life, I actually feel hope that I might be saved. I've just seen how gracious God is."

Yet at the same time that somebody sitting in a pew is falling to her knees to praise God, others are picking up stones. Consider, for example, the woman who shouted at me as I left a church one Sabbath morning: "You've left out the most important part!"

"I've just spent an hour showing you the significance of the death and resurrection of Jesus," I replied.

"But," she protested, "you've left out *my* role in all this."

"Well," I answered, "I hate to tell you this, sister, but you should fall down and repent immediately, if you think that you are capable of doing something that will earn you the favor and the righteousness of God."

Let's face it—Christians haven't always done that well in helping people see the grace of God. Every now and again we witness a breakthrough, when people realize they are liberated and free in Jesus. Yet others start calling them liberals, simply because they now realize that the grace of God could never be earned—that it is given to anyone freely. The discovery of free grace should not automatically place the believer in the liberal camp, as if somehow, they are now in danger of suddenly running out to break all the rules.

The Faithful Waldenses

Disagreements over grace became a life-and-death struggle for the Christian Church—and the light of truth almost went out. Little groups of faithful people such as the Waldenses hid in caves to escape persecution for their unyielding belief in God's grace. But even these loyal ones were ultimately deceived. They were tricked.

The high mountain valleys where the Waldenses retreated were located in northern Italy and southern France. Narrow entrances to the valleys made them easy to defend.

But an emissary of the pope sent them a message that if they would allow the papal representative to come in, the Waldenses would be given religious liberty and freedom. Well, it didn't happen. They allowed the emissary to come in, but they lost their freedom and liberty in the process. It's a very sad story.

The light of truth almost went out! And had there not been an expedition across to the New World, I think the light might indeed have gone out! But God wasn't prepared to have the light go out. Even a handful of believers was enough, and He sent them across to the New World so that the light of truth could be understood again in these last days.

Without doubt, the Reformation was the single most significant event in the history of Christianity since the birth of Jesus!

Jesus came to bring light into a world that for 4,000 years had been shrouded in pagan darkness. Yet before too long, the people of the world were again being taught that they must do everything possible to appease God—to cause Him to feel better toward them. What a terrible counterfeit of the truth! What a perversion of the truth of God's free grace!

CHAPTER TWO

Two Views of Salvation

What is the biggest—the most important—Catholic sacrament?

What do they call it? The *mass.* Yes, the mass is the number-one sacrament. And who is the key player in the mass? The priest—who has authority to command the Son of God to come down and enter into the wafer. What an elevated position for a priest to be in! Incredible! The mass is the number-one sacrament, because it's celebrated several times a day in most churches.

But as the Reformation drew near, God reached a point where He said, "Enough!"

And what enabled God finally to say, "Enough!"? What development enabled Him to say, "I'm going to let the light start to shine?"

The printing press was definitely a big factor. But the biggest factor was that finally, God found Himself a man! You know, I've wondered for years whether God, in fact, didn't have a man for all those hundreds of years. That's a scary thought, you know? Was there no Joshua, no Elijah? Perhaps He had to wait. But what a man He finally had on His hands—rough, coarse—but a man who was serious about God and His Word and prepared to act on it!

You know, when Martin Luther turned and walked out of that assembly at the Diet of Worms—it has been said there's never been a more glittering assembly of kings and priests and cardinals and bishops ever assembled on this earth—when he turned and walked out, I think that's one of the greatest moments in history.

Luther turned his back and just walked out, unharmed—and, as you may know the story, was taken by the elector of Saxony and hidden in a castle, where he spent his time translating the New Testament into German. Wow!

I don't think Catholicism had a clue what could happen once the Bible was printed in the languages of the common people.

We think Luther was the biggest factor, but perhaps the printed Word was probably the number one factor. It really took both the Word and a man who would unchain it for the common people.

And the great issue of the Reformation—as we noted in the previous chapter—focused on grace. The Catholic Church maintained that grace could be earned, or even purchased. It held that an intermediate step between God and a believer was necessary in order to receive it.

I know people who believe they're being born again when they are baptized. It's not true, of course, but the reason I'm introducing this to you now is because it helps set the stage for what we're going to encounter in later chapters as we move into Romans.

Two ideologies, or theories, of salvation developed out of the Reformation. On one side were the teachings of the reformer Jean Calvin. He was a great man of God. And while you may not agree (I don't) with everything he taught—a view of truth called Calvinism—he wrote some stirring things. I've never read a better exposition of baptism in my life than in the writings of Calvin.

On the other hand we have what is known as Arminianism. Calvinism and Arminianism set forth two contrasting schools of thought.

Seventh-day Adventists have traditionally seen themselves as on the side of Arminianism, not on the side of Calvinism. And I'll explain to you what that means in a moment.

So how were these two schools of thought different?

Calvinism says that God made provision for salvation at the cross—that He didn't save anybody at the cross but just made *provision* for salvation. But Calvinism goes farther and says that even God's provision for salvation was not for everyone—only, instead, for just "the elect."

One of the biggest theories associated with Calvinism is the theory of predestination—the idea that God chose only certain people to be saved. That's how we think of Calvinism—God only planned to redeem certain people. You can imagine the picture of God that lies behind this. God only planned to redeem a handful of people—the elect. And they were the only ones for whom the provision for salvation was made at the cross.

Calvinists have a problem with certain texts of Scripture. For example:

▶ John 12:32: "And I, if I am lifted up from the earth, will draw **all** men to Myself."

▶ John 3:16: "For God so loved the world, that He gave His only begotten Son, that **whoever** believes in Him shall not perish, but have eternal life."

▶ 2 Peter 3:9: "The Lord is not slow about His promise, as some count slowness, but is patient toward you, not wishing for any to perish but for **all** to come to repentance."

Calvinism has a serious struggle with such texts. They are known as "universalist" texts, because they appear to show that God made provision for universal salvation, in contrast with the salvation of an elite elect. Calvinism, by the way, is a very disillusioning philosophy, if you conclude that you are not among the elect. Imagine if you were considered not to be among the elect!

It's interesting that the Jehovah's Witnesses seem to maintain a similar belief. You have probably never met a Jehovah's Witness who has a heavenly hope. Have you ever met one who is planning to go to heaven? Most Jehovah's Witnesses will tell you they're not planning to go to heaven—that heaven is strictly reserved only for the 144,000. These members have no heavenly hope whatsoever. It's kind of a variation on the Calvinist theme.

I feel almost sad for them when I talk to them about this. I've never met one yet who has any hope of heaven. I ask every one I meet, and they all say, "No, no—I'm not going, but I know someone who is." And I say to myself, "Wow." Imagine being in church, and here's someone who's been identified as among the elect, and everyone else around this person has no heavenly hope. That's what it's like. These members think they're going to be a part of an effort to reclaim the earth and bring it back for better times—not a terrible existence, but it's just not the joy of going to be with God. That's reserved for—it's the privilege of—only a handful.

So that's one side—one of the views of salvation—and Seventh-day Adventism as a movement was never in this camp, for obvious reasons.

A Better View?

Now, the other side took a much stronger stand. This side said that God didn't simply make provision for salvation at the cross but that He actually redeemed man at the cross. So it was not a provision—it was a redemption—that took place at the cross.

But—even this "better" view of salvation had its limitations, by saying that salvation depends upon man's ability to repent and confess, rather than on the sublime fact that God permitted His Son, "who knew no sin to be sin on our behalf, so that we might become the righteousness of God in Him" 2 Corinthians 5:21. Are you beginning to notice something?

That God actually did redeem mankind at the cross sounds totally wonderful to begin with. He paid the price—and we certainly have no problem with that.

But then this "better" view goes on to say—and to say it emphatically—that salvation is absolutely dependent on man's ability to repent and confess. So what are you noticing? What are you hearing?

What we are actually hearing here is Catholicism served up in Protestant dress. What we are hearing is a subtle restatement of Catholic theology: "If I can do this…or this…I will be deserving of the grace of God—of His salvation. But only as long as I do this… or this…" It's *my* repentance. *My* confession. *My* good works.

And here, the Advent movement took issue with Arminianism. You can see why they were more on the Arminian side of the disagreement over salvation, because they loved what was being said about redemption on the cross. But they took issue with what was added to that thought—the idea that man was still the key factor here. He still has to *do* something.

I know many people, by the way, who believe that unless they can confess something, they're not forgiven. I hope you didn't miss those words. I know many people who believe that unless they can confess something—or everything, really—they will never be forgiven. That is another form of the key Arminian error.

Confession, after all, is not something we do in order to receive the grace of God, but is instead a demonstration—a "fruit"— showing that the grace of God has come into your life.

For example, I'm rather fascinated that in Scripture, repentance is given to the children of God—it's God's gift to His own children. Confession too is an evidence that the grace of God has come into my life. And I'm now open with God, because I'm enjoying a relationship with Him—and I don't keep secrets from somebody with whom I want a healthy relationship. But it's so easy to turn confession around and make it the means of receiving the grace of God.

This view of things is all too common among Christians. I know people who keep the Sabbath, for example, because they believe that if they don't keep it a certain way, they will be lost. In other words, the way they keep the Sabbath determines whether or not they receive the grace of God. But in actual fact, the way they keep the Sabbath is a reflection of whether or not the grace of God has entered into them!

The Jews, as you may know, had over 600 rules in the Mishnah. The reason God finally said to the Jews, "I'm taking the kingdom from you, and giving it to a people who were once not My people" (see Romans 9:25, 26) and took from them the privilege of revealing Himself to the world was because they were perpetuating a system that said, "If you observe these 600 ways of keeping the Sabbath, you will be guaranteed the favor of God."

God's grace and favor come to us as a free gift. We can't say that enough. We do not earn it. We do not deserve it. We do not work for it. We do not make ourselves good enough for it. It's ours, free—is that not a relief? Is that not good news?

CHAPTER THREE

The Line Between Faith and Works

There's a world of difference between keeping the Sabbath because you're enjoying a saved relationship with God—and keeping it instead because you hope that by doing so, maybe God will feel better toward you, so you'll have His smile and not His frown.

There's a great deal you can do that simply reveals that you have already received salvation—instead of doing things in order to earn or deserve salvation. It's a wonderful experience to get to a place where you finally realize there is not a single thing that you can "do" to be saved.

It is so easy to cross the line between faith and works. I even know people who are self-righteous about their understanding of righteousness by faith! I'm serious! They are so proud of the fact that their understanding of this great truth is so much greater than everybody else's, that they've crossed the line from faith… into works.

This is quite likely the greatest danger faced, not only by Adventists, but by all Christians in the Protestant tradition. Protestantism broke away from this, and that is what made it such a remarkable, powerful movement.

Faith. Some people think that because of faith, they have nothing to do. But my experience tells me that entering into a life of constant faith is a pretty big challenge. I constantly have to check my motives—to be sure I'm not doing some good thing in order to get more of God's grace, but rather that I'm doing good or obeying because of my deep gratitude for the grace He's already offered me. Now, I'm more than willing—I'm eager—to do whatever God says is pleasing to Him.

I've been looking at people for years and asking, "Why do people have such a problem doing what God says is pleasing to Him?"

And I've found the answer to that question. If I have to do good things in order to guarantee that God will feel good toward me, then ultimately, I'm going to hate God. He's made my life miserable. That's what I've concluded after years of watching people who try to find ways around what God says is pleasing to Him. Sometimes they'll even ask for my support or approval to do this. And I look at them almost with pity. Because they're still not seeing how gracious God has been in Jesus Christ!

You can always tell when somebody hasn't really, fully seen God's graciousness, because they will approach you and say, "Oh, you know, it's so hard. I'm struggling with this, and this, and this." And you know the one thing they never mention? It's what God has done in Christ.

Instead, they're so overwhelmed with their circumstances, their problems, their challenges, and the difficulties of living, that you never hear them talk about what God has done in Christ. What they're really saying is, "I'm not making it, and God isn't feeling very good toward me. So I may as well just go out and blow it." How many hundreds of people have I heard say this! Because they don't think God feels very good about them, they don't feel good about God!

I wasn't reared as a Christian, as some of you may know, so my own thinking was not along those lines—and I praise God for that.

We so much need to be really clear about this relationship

The Line Between Faith and Works • 25

between faith and works—between doing good so God will save us, and doing good from gratitude that He already has! If we are confused about this, we risk falling into the same pattern as the Jews of Bible times. And if that happens, we forfeit the privilege of revealing God to the world. Because the truth of God's grace is again, just what we noted in the previous chapter.

God's grace can't be earned.

We can't do anything to deserve it.

It's not a reward for doing right.

It's not a payment for obedience.

It's not based on anything we "do."

Grace is based on what Jesus did. It's ours even if we don't deserve it. And God doesn't wait to see if we will obey and "do right" before He gives us the free gift of grace.

Is this good news? Is this not the best news ever?

CHAPTER FOUR

Means—or Fruit?

If people don't find the grace of God in a church that claims to be walking in the light, what then?

They may go looking elsewhere.

They may become disillusioned.

Or they may give up totally.

Now, I don't think the members of the Seventh-day Adventist Church need to lace up their walking shoes and start out on a guilt trip, because not only does this Church claim to be walking in the light, but millions have indeed found God's grace through the Church and its members.

Looking at the history of Adventists as a people, we know that they are a product of Protestantism. The Adventist Church was at first comprised of Lutherans, Baptists, Methodists, Catholics, and others—all of whom came out of their former spiritual homes and joined together in excitement over end-time prophecy. So Adventists truly are the fruit of the Protestant movement.

But unfortunately—and I have a great burden about this—it would appear that many Adventists, some naively, some inadvertently, and some ignorantly, are drifting into a mindset that says that if they don't "do" this, or don't measure up in this… or this….or even this…God will not feel good toward them. He will not be pleased or happy with them.

And sadly, some Adventists, while under the shadow of this kind of thinking, find that a holy life eludes them. Why? Because a holy life is possessed only by those who see and respond to the free grace of God. So it becomes something of a "Catch-22."

So we find that we must carefully distinguish between the "means" and the "fruit." There's a world of difference here—everything hinges on those two words.

Are we doing the good things we do—are we obeying God—as a *means* of receiving His grace? Or are we doing them because the grace of God has already been freely given to us through Jesus Christ?

Take repentance, for example. It's not something I have to do in order for God to feel good toward me. I repent because I don't want to keep secrets from someone who has loved me so infinitely much. I want to be an open book.

Means and *fruit*—they are worlds apart. And *fruit* is the product of yet another word: *free*. I do what I do because I am saved freely.

In studying the book of Romans, it's vital that we understand this issue as Paul did. And Paul did indeed clearly understand the difference between *means* and *fruit*. It set him apart from nearly every other person in New Testament times. He was single-eyed in his focus. And what was that focus? The things he had to do to earn God's grace? No—"For I determined to know nothing among you except Jesus Christ and Him crucified." 1 Corinthians 2:2. Paul saw it clearly.

We can't allow ourselves to get caught in the trap of a dualistic understanding, in which, on the one hand, God does something beautiful on the cross—yet salvation somehow still hinges on our human ability to do this, this…or this.

What is the result of that kind of thinking?

The result is tragic: we remain slaves to sin. Paul devotes a whole chapter to helping us understand this to be the result of confusing *means* with *fruit*. We remain slaves to sin, so that the very thing we long to be free of is denied to us. Because freedom from sin simply is not possible—we cannot achieve it—without the grace of God in our hearts.

When we discover that we cannot break free from sin, we may very well become angry toward God. Angry, because we are still prisoners to sin. Angry, because God seems to have set before us impossible conditions to meet in order to be saved.

Not only may we become angry, but discouraged as well. And be practical—be honest with me now. Just how discouraged may we get? Ultimately, we may become so discouraged we abandon ourselves to total rebellion. But before that, we may experience something else. We will lack assurance—any security at all about our salvation.

This leads us to a "yo-yo" spiritual experience, in which—at least as we experience it—we fall in and out of grace, in and out of salvation. We make a mistake—and we believe we've fallen out of grace.

Free to Make a Mistake

Imagine that! I've made a mistake, so I conclude that God no longer feels good toward me. So how do I regain His favor? I must rectify the mistake. Unfortunately, the harder I try to rectify it, the deeper a hole I dig for myself. Because unless my heart is born anew, I simply can't rectify my mistakes—it's just not in me. I've been born in iniquity—conceived in sin. Psalm 51:5. With an inborn propensity toward evil, even when I want to do good, I find that evil is present within me, trying to take me another way. Romans 7:21.

So imagine if my having the grace of God was dependent—only, ever, and always—on my ability to do the right thing. You know, the day it finally hit me that under the grace of God, *there is freedom actually to make a mistake,* I was overwhelmed! You mean to say that I could actually make a mistake and not lose the grace of God?

It was as if God took out a big baseball bat and hit me with the amazing truth of it. "Open your eyes," He said. "My grace has never depended on your ability to do the right thing. My grace was offered to you even while you were yet a sinner."

Sometimes the word *wow* has its place—and here's one of them!

Some of you may spend years of your life moving in and out of grace—in and out of salvation. And every time you slip up, you'll try to find a way of somehow making it right. Yet you discover you can't.

I myself spent years in that yo-yo experience. And every time I made a mistake, I just didn't know how I would ever get back in the grace of God again. Because I wasn't good enough—I wasn't consistent enough. It was so discouraging—so depressing.

I almost left Christianity over this issue, I'm serious. I actually said to God one day—I went out and shouted at Him, "It doesn't work!"

And He said it again: "Open your eyes! I'm not asking the impossible of *you*. I asked it of *Jesus*!"

God finally got through to me.

"I'm not asking you to *be* Jesus," He said—and I thought, "Oh, what a relief!"

"No, I'm just asking you to *believe* in Jesus."

If your focus is on your own human performance, or even worse, if it's on somebody else's performance, you will have no hope. You'll have the yo-yo experience, you'll go up and down, you'll move in and out of grace, you'll move in and out of salvation, and more and more, you will begin to feel hopeless.

There's no joy, there's no peace, there's no assurance, there's no relationship in this kind of experience! How can you have a relationship with a God who saves you only if you always do the right thing—even as everything in you is pulling you toward sin?

We have not been kind to God, you know. And it's robbed so many precious people of any assurance of salvation—just so very many. This is not true only of Adventists, not at all. That's why it's a great miracle to me that a Catholic priest on his knees—at least that's the tradition, of Luther going up those Spanish Steps there in Rome (and they're still there)—heard a voice in His mind. And the Spirit of the Lord said to him, "The just shall live by faith!"

And Luther got back to his study, took out his pen, and wrote in the margin of his Bible, alongside Romans 1:16 and 17, the Latin word *sola*, which means "alone."

"The just shall live by faith, *alone!*"

How many people do I know who have begun their journey by faith, yet ended it mired in the hopelessness of human effort and works?

Yet someday, for many, it finally comes clear: "I'm not capable of even one pure thought, one generous action, one unselfish desire. I don't have the capacity to generate one ounce of holiness. My best efforts are comparable to filthy rags."

That's my *best* efforts. How could I ever start believing that there's something I could ever do to convince God to feel better toward me? I can't. And the good news is, *I don't have to!* Because, while we were yet sinners, Christ died for us. While we were helpless, while we were enemies, He loved us! Romans 5:6-10.

That's grace.

And once you see it, you are never the same again. You'll never take credit for anything decent that is manifested in your life, because you will know it's the grace of God—it's not you! Any noble impulse, generous deed, pure thought—it's all God in you, not you.

"The just shall live by faith."

By faith *alone*.

CHAPTER FIVE

The Source of Our Peace

I got so angry with God once I told Him I wasn't going to work for Him any more. "I'm not going to tell anybody else about You," I said.

One thing I like about God is that He must have an incredible sense of humor. Because the next morning, He brought a young sergeant from the Army in full uniform, who knocked on my door.

"Yes?" I answered.

"Well," he replied, "somebody told me that if I came to you, you would help me find salvation."

"You've come to the wrong place," I told him. "I can't help you. I need help myself!"

"Well, somebody told me that you would help me!"

"Well, bully for you!" I answered angrily.

"Please!" the young sergeant pled. "I'm lost!"

And do you know what? I could not resist. I proceeded to show him the path of salvation. That night, I went out and stood under the stars and repented.

"Forgive me, God," I said, "for such foolish thinking on my part."

"Don't forget," He replied. "I spoke through a donkey once—I'm not limited!"

"Thanks a lot!" I answered.

We've all had our moments. But do you know what God told me after my experience that night?

"I hope you realize that you haven't fallen out of grace over this," His voice seemed to say to me.

"That's overwhelming," I responded. "How could You continue to love me?"

"Because," He replied, "My love is not based on whether or not you always do the right thing. I love you. I loved you when you were yet a sinner, when you were rebellious, when you were an enemy, when you were helpless! I love, because I AM love. I don't love because you've done something good. The truth is, if you've done something good, it really isn't you! It's me!"

How little I understand the grace of God, I thought.

How's your faith at this moment?

On one hand, we see works of *faith*. On the other, we see—in the words of Paul—works of...what?

Works of *law*.

When Paul uses the expression *works of law*, he's talking about works—things you do in an effort to receive the grace of God.

Works of faith, on the other hand, are things seen in your life as a result of receiving the grace of God.

Why do you think Martin Luther had a problem with the book of James? He called it a "right strawy" epistle. "Strawy." It's a funny-sounding word, isn't it? That was Luther's description of the epistle of James. In other words, it's nothing solid.

But Luther, brilliant as he was, failed to see that James was describing works of faith—"faith without works is dead" (James 2:26)—whereas

Paul was working with the legalistic Jews, so he was dealing with works as they related to law.

Paul had a whole nation around him which was trying to demonstrate to God that it deserved His grace. Those who belonged to this nation—as they saw it—were more righteous, more holy, more pure. But they really weren't!

So Luther misunderstood James, interestingly enough. For a long while, he wouldn't even read it. And after he read it, he threw it away. Even the great Reformation master himself failed to see that James was looking at works simply from the other side of the coin. James spoke of works, not as a means of saving you but as a demonstration of the faith that you have.

Avoiding the Extremes

It's vital to understand the true relationship between faith and works. It's vital to understand God's free grace. It's vital to see salvation and righteousness in a balanced way, avoiding extremes.

By the grace of God, Seventh-day Adventist pioneers, as they struggled to understand these great Bible truths, were saved from the pitfalls—the extremes—of both Calvinism and Arminianism. Even though those pioneers found the Arminian position more in harmony with the Word, they did not accept that man could in any way earn the grace of God.

Unfortunately—tragically, even—many Adventists have now slipped fully into the errors contained in Arminianism, and they're doing things—even good things—from the wrong motives!

There's no freedom in that. There's no joy. There's no peace.

By the way, the struggles of the early Advent pioneers to learn truth were amazing! Those early believers stayed up all night sometimes wrestling with these issues. But I think it's miraculous that God was able to bring together Advent believers from Baptist, Methodist, Lutheran, Catholic, and Anglican faiths—and after they'd all been praying and discussing together, they avoided the pitfalls of Arminianism. They took the good from it and ended up with a magnificent understanding of righteousness by faith.

But that understanding didn't come clear until 1888. So it took forty-four years for the early believers to clarify the issues of righteousness by faith and avoid the errors found in Arminianism. To these early believers, it was like coming out of the Dark Ages again.

We Can't Earn Grace

By the way, there's a very good reason why we can't earn the grace of God. And that reason is that He couldn't give more grace to us than He's already given! That's why we can't earn more. God has given us freely ALL that His grace has to offer.

It took forty-four years for this understanding to come through clearly. Yet this struggle goes on today. It's not over. The message has been clarified repeatedly. Have you noticed—especially over the last twenty or thirty years—the number of those who have arisen focusing us again on the completeness of righteousness by faith? This is not by accident! God appears very determined to make sure that none of His own children miss the opportunity of coming to the understanding of how absolutely generous and gracious He has been in Jesus Christ.

So ask yourselves a big question. Are you trying to do anything to earn, or purchase, or prove to God that you are deserving of salvation? Ask yourself that question right now. Just think about your life—your lifestyle.

Because if you are trying in any way to earn or deserve salvation, Romans is going to confront you boldly. Are you doing any single thing because of a desire to obtain the goodness of God, the grace of God, the approval of God—to impress Him with how much you've grown, how well you're doing, or how deserving you are of salvation? Anything at all?

If you are, you've slipped into an age-old philosophy which has largely controlled the minds of the inhabitants of this earth through nearly all of human history.

And if you are, the apostle Paul, in Romans 5:1, wants to challenge you. Even though the world will tell you that you can have peace of mind by taking a seminar that teaches you to look within yourself, or that maybe you can contact some of your dead ancestors, or perhaps make some adjustments in your relationships—peace with God comes *only* through our Lord Jesus Christ.

So if you're lacking peace in your life right now, it's because Jesus is not central to your life.

I want these words to ring in your minds: "Having been justified by faith, we now have peace." Romans 5:1.

Some of you may know that *justification* is a printer's term. When both the left and right sides of a column of type line up perfectly straight, they are said to be justified. They are "set" in perfect vertical alignment.

The basic theological meaning of the word in Greek, the original language of the New Testament, is "justified," or "declared." Not *"made* righteous," but *"declared* righteous." Another way of putting it, if we think of the paper illustration, is "set right."

The incredibly Good News is—and notice the tense here: "having been"—it's an accomplished fact. Yes, it is *"having been* justified by faith, we have peace with God through our Lord Jesus Christ."

So the faith is tied together with Jesus! It's through Jesus! God has done something in Jesus that has enabled Him to set you right. You are the column of typeset words. Put up against a straightedge—which is like God's standard of righteousness—the words are in perfect alignment. They are justified. And so are you! And I want to tell you that you will never, ever, be able to add to or improve upon that standard.

In the sight of God you are as holy as Jesus Himself is holy. You are totally in conformity to the complete law of God in Jesus Christ. That's how God sees you.

And according to Paul, this is our source of peace. Having enough money in the bank? That's not the source. I know people who've got plenty of money in the bank, and they have no peace. Having all the possessions this world can offer? That's not the source of peace—not at all.

Peace is knowing and believing that whatever God did through Jesus enables Him to take your column of words and put them up against His perfect rule—His standard of righteousness—and declare you to be as perfect as He is.

When you see that standard, you despair that you can ever line up perfectly and be justified. But God says, "In Jesus, you already *have* been justified."

This is an incredible thing!

Truly incredible.

CHAPTER SIX

Salvation—Accomplished Fact and Ongoing Process

Prepare now, in this brief chapter, for a major statement—something God showed the pioneers of the advent movement. It's God's gift to the Seventh-day Adventist Church of a truth so powerful that I praise Him for it every day.

Here it is: Salvation, wrote the Apostle Paul, is both an *accomplished fact* ("having been justified")—and an *ongoing process*.

We often tell people that they can come to Jesus just as they are, but I always tell them, "Count the cost, because you will not remain as God finds you. The moment you come by faith and believe what God did in Jesus to save you, then that already-accomplished salvation enters into you through the Holy Spirit, and you partake of life. You are never the same again."

This is very important. That's why we find Paul's incredible emphasis on both the death and the resurrection of Jesus. Christ's death is the means by which we partake of His life—and it's all ours by faith.

Quite frankly, until we allow ourselves to see that salvation is an already-accomplished fact, we are generally robbed of the privilege of the ongoing process. Because Christ's life is only given to those who see what God has done through Christ's death.

So do you see why this is such a major statement—such a powerful idea?

Some people want just *part* of the salvation God has provided. They want the benefits of Christ's death—then seem to want to stop there. They want the accomplished fact of salvation but don't see the importance of the ongoing process. But we need the whole package to experience salvation fully.

Salvation is not a passive experience. Yes, it is based on an accomplished fact. But when we really take hold of that fact, the very life of Jesus—the same life He lived here on Earth—enters into us, and we grow up into Christ.

So when we find people who've become Christians, yet have no victory in their lives and are not experiencing the ongoing process—what do we know already? We know that they have failed to see what is an accomplished fact. And failure to see and appreciate what Jesus accomplished on the cross is the single biggest factor that denies people the privilege of being connected to the vine.

A failure to appreciate what Jesus accomplished at the cross prevents us from fully understanding how salvation happens. That's why perhaps the best habit we each could develop would be to spend a thoughtful hour every day focusing on that cross, looking at what Jesus really accomplished there in human flesh.

Paul first focuses on the already-accomplished fact of salvation—what Jesus achieved for us at the cross. Then he opens the door for us to move into understanding the second part of salvation—the ongoing process.

Accomplished fact. Ongoing process. Salvation includes them both. Why? Because both are found in the one Man, Jesus Christ. And when we receive Jesus, we receive not just what He has already

Salvation—Accomplished Fact and Ongoing Process • 41

done for us, but also what He continues to do when He comes to live out His overcoming life in us through the Holy Spirit.

Another way to look at it is this: We cannot rejoice in the gift of Jesus as our Savior from sin—without also embracing Him as our Lord and Master. He is both. So when we invite Jesus into our hearts and lives, we receive not only His *pardon* for our sin—but also the *power* of His resurrected life to obey His will for us.

There's a reason the Gospel is called Good News!

CHAPTER SEVEN

The Truth That Shakes the World

Salvation, as noted in the previous chapter, has two parts: what Jesus already accomplished for us at the cross—and the ongoing process of what He accomplishes in us.

It's vital that we clearly understand what the Bible teaches us about salvation—and perhaps no other Bible writer has made it as plain as did the Apostle Paul in the book of Romans. Hundreds of years after Paul, his clear presentation of the magnificent and free grace of God would emerge as the key to meeting centuries of error with truth.

In this chapter, I want to revisit now a time we've touched on already in earlier chapters—a time when the Bible truth about salvation was taught and preached with unprecedented power. That pivotal time has come to be called the Reformation.

For a thousand years and more prior to the Reformation, Catholicism dominated the religious scene. Though the Catholic Church contained many precious seekers after truth, the Church's system of false teachings plunged the world into darkness. Why? Because it was based on the philosophy that sinners could in some way earn or purchase grace.

A whole system was established wherein sinners were taught to come through the priest and partake of the sacraments in order to receive God's grace. The Mass, of course, was the chief sacrament. Another significant sacrament focused on the stations of the cross, in which believers knelt and counted their rosaries before each station. Another means of obtaining grace was through indulgences—paying fees to reduce a member's term in purgatory by thousands of years. The confessional, also, was yet another means of obtaining grace.

I'd like to suggest that we don't confess in order to receive the grace of God. Rather, we confess because we have *already* freely received His grace! And I'd also like to suggest that when we fall back into sin, we don't confess or even repent in order to regain God's favor, because it is already and freely ours!

This is not a popular teaching with many Seventh-day Adventists, because they've been raised to think if you do the right thing, you will have the favor of God. And perhaps the majority of people that I relate with are in that camp.

So God in His infinite wisdom raised up a man named Martin Luther, an unlikely man—a rough, coarse, Catholic, married monk—but a stubborn man and a man of great spirit. Tradition says he was walking up the Spanish Steps in Rome on his knees, when he heard the voice of God say—quoting Romans 1:16 and 17—"The just shall live by faith!"

And why was Luther walking up the steps on his knees? To do penance, so that he could earn the privilege of having God looking favorably upon him again. And he stopped, according to tradition, halfway up the steps and said, "What am I doing? If the just shall live by faith, why am I crawling up here trying to convince God that I'm worthy of something?"

So he went home and wrote in the margin of his Bible, alongside those verses, the Latin word *sola*—which means "alone." The just shall live by faith *alone*, apart from the works of the law!

So after 1,300 years of darkness in the Church, Luther saw the light! He didn't realize, of course, that he was about to take on the whole Catholic system. He never planned to do that. He just got excited as everyone does when they realize what the free grace of God is—that you don't have to spend your life convincing God of something which, in fact, you know is not true about yourself! That's what it amounts to. Luther was liberated.

"Here I Stand"

Outside of the birth and death of Jesus Christ, I don't think there's been a greater moment in history than when Luther stood boldly for his faith. Before the most august assembly imaginable—kings, rulers, the bishops, emperors—Luther stood at the Diet of Worms and simply stated his convictions: "You can accuse me of anything you like," he said in essence. "But I'm standing on the Word of God. Here I stand—I can do no other. And if the Word of God says that His grace is free, then it's free. And that means that our whole religious system is contrary to God's Word."

Of course, God was with Luther, and the elector of Saxony hid him away in a castle for years, where Luther translated the New Testament into German and put it into the hands of the people. Perhaps Luther's greatest contribution of all was in making the Bible available, not just to church leaders, but to everyone.

So it was that Protestantism was formed. And out of Protestantism came two major streams of thought. One was called Calvinism—the other Arminianism. Traditionally, Seventh-day Adventists have been on the side of Arminianism.

Calvinism taught that God didn't actually redeem anybody at the cross—but that instead, He only made *provision* for salvation. And even then, that provision was reserved for only a handful of people—the very elect. In other words, everyone else was basically damned.

The Advent movement has never bought into Calvinism, the teachings of which ultimately, of course, led to the doctrine of predestination.

The so-called "universalist" texts are a great problem to

Calvinists, because those Scriptures teach that salvation is for all men—that whosoever will, may come—that salvation is for as many as believe.

On the other side of the debate, the Arminian theory had much to recommend it. Because Arminianism said, "No, God just didn't make provision at the cross—He actually redeemed sinners at the cross." This, of course, we adhere to.

But—and this is where Arminianism deviated a little from the clarity of the gospel and it's teachings on grace—Arminianism taught that salvation depends on man's ability to confess and repent.

So once again, this time wearing the garment of Protestantism rather than Catholicism, we have a movement teaching that grace can be purchased, if I am able to confess or repent.

And how can you know whether or not you're buying into that idea? You could hear me wax eloquently for an hour about the death of Jesus Christ, for example, and be sitting there saying, "But what's my part in all this?"

But if that's what you're saying to yourself, you're still missing the boat, because until we can get out of the way sufficiently to allow ourselves to see how gracious God has been in Jesus Christ—to see what He's already given us freely through the death of Christ—then, even if we reach out and take hold of it, it will never truly be a blessing to us if we're not also seeing what God is freely offering us through the life of Christ.

So please don't be hung up on what our role is in this. Of course, our role is to take hold by faith of what He has already given and also what He is offering us.

But I've got news for you. Even *that* is the gift of God! That's the grace of God. And when we understand what grace is all about, we will never, ever, be seeking credit, in any respect, for any spiritual growth that has taken place within us. We will recognize that God has given His grace despite us, apart from us, while we were, in fact, yet sinners.

So anytime—and I'm very serious now—anytime you hear about or practice a theology which gives us any degree of credit for the good that is happening within us, you can be confident that you've slipped back to a form of Catholicism, even though it may have a sweet-sounding Protestant name.

It could even be called Seventh-day Adventism! Any teaching or preaching—even in the Adventist Church—that grace is dependent upon the human ability to respond, is not the Bible truth about salvation.

What a remarkable moment it was in history when Martin Luther saw this Bible truth clearly. After being part of a system that had dominated the world for 1,300 years, for Luther actually to see that he was buying into a teaching about grace that was not Biblical was a truly incredible thing! And of course, God gets all the glory for that pivotal moment too.

When Luther discovered the truth of free salvation by grace, it shook the entire religious world. When you and I rediscover it today, it shakes our world as well.

CHAPTER EIGHT

Adventists and Righteousness By Faith

Seventh-day Adventism, as noted in the previous chapter, has been the recipient of much grace from God, because the pioneers of the Advent movement recognized that they were on the Arminian rather than the Calvinistic side of the Reformation debate about salvation. But these pioneers didn't feel comfortable with everything that Arminianism taught.

So the Spirit of God led the Advent movement to avoid the pitfalls and to come to an understanding that man, in fact, could not save himself. But it took them forty-four years to clarify the understanding of righteousness by faith. Let that thought penetrate.

It took the earliest participants in this movement, founded by the most sincere and zealous people from every church coming together to search the Word—it took them forty-four years to clarify the issue of how we are saved. And that's after Luther paved the way and after many other great saints wrote on it and studied it. It still took forty-four years to get it clear that righteousness is a free gift.

What's another word for righteousness? Holiness. And whether that righteousness is *imputed*—with God graciously saying, "I'm going to credit you with perfect righteousness. I'm going to treat you like a holy person"—or whether it's *imparted,* where you're actually experiencing the presence of the Spirit within you and the mind of God being given to you—it's always 100 percent the righteousness of Jesus Christ.

There is never a time when man has been able to manufacture his little portion. It's always the righteousness of Jesus.

A Continuing Struggle

And this led to a most intense struggle in the Adventist Church. Because the leadership of the movement in 1888 was not favorable to the full truth of righteousness by faith, even though Ellen White, the servant of the Lord herself, wrote affirming what A. T. Jones and E. J. Waggoner were preaching and teaching, because they saw this light. Of course, it came to them from God.

The leadership still positioned itself against the light taking hold, and it took many years after 1888 for it to become an established and recognized part of this movement. Have you noticed how the Adventist Church still struggles with it? And why do you think there is such an intense struggle over the issue of righteousness by faith? Because it's a human tendency to want some of the credit. We think we need to do something.

Many churches encounter struggles, of course. One of the big denominations at the moment is having a struggle concerning ordaining homosexuals into the priesthood. That's a big struggle. And other churches are having different types of struggles.

The Church of Jesus Christ of Latter-day Saints went through a huge struggle as to whether blacks could ever really be saved or be a part of the priesthood. Because God hadn't given them a revelation on it yet, you know. Then one day, according to them, God changed His mind and gave them a revelation.

Yes, other churches go through different struggles, but the Adventist Church since 1888 has gone through a continuing series of struggles in the attempt to clarify righteousness by faith.

I can think of different men God has raised up in the last twenty or thirty years to preach and teach about it. Some people in the Church have said, "Oh, praise the Lord! For the first time in my life I feel free in Christ! I'm not free to go out and sin—but I'm free to rejoice now with an assurance of salvation."

But others in the Church have as much as said, "Get out the guns! Let's shoot them down!"

I'm fascinated by how much feeling there is on this subject! And you can notice it even today. Just preach in a local church on these matters, and you're going to have some people falling down on their faces praising God—and others will be looking at you, saying, "Well, when did *you* leave the Adventist Church?"

I'm serious! Because this struggle is rooted in the selfish, natural, human heart. And the natural heart wants some recognition—some credit.

Christianity, in contrast to all teachings of modern and pop psychology, tells people it's OK to accept the fact that you are worthless—that sin has made you worthless, useless, incapable of helping yourself.

And how grateful we should be that God doesn't consider us worthless! He sees value there. And He even sacrificed His own Son. But it's OK to acknowledge the fact that I am a worm! "Woe is me, I'm a man of unclean lips, because my eyes have seen the glory of the Lord!" Isaiah 6:5.

And if you've seen the glory of the Lord, you'll never be hung up on seeking recognition, affirmation, or credit for somehow making an incredible difference, because anything you've ever done has always been Christ in you.

"Not I," said Paul, "but Christ, who lives within me." Galatians 2:20.

Here's the strongest man in the New Testament—yet he can't and won't take one ounce of credit for himself.

Of course, buying into Arminianism, as many Seventh-day Adventists have and still do, has left some with no assurance. They get angry toward God, they're still slaves of sin, they're lacking joy and peace, and they end up in the "yo-yo" experience. They move in and out of grace. And if they fall back, or make a mistake, or get involved in sin, what do they start believing?

"I'm out of grace. I'm lost."

This is common—very common today.

When this happens, you end up saying, "Who cares? I'm never going to be good enough, so why should I even persevere?"

And that's based on not understanding that the grace of God has never hinged on how good you are! Because you are not good by nature! You've never been able to earn it, buy it, or do something to deserve it! It is absolutely free!

The reason we don't have to convince God to feel better toward us is that He's already given everything He could give!

So the Seventh-day Adventist movement is truly unique in this world. And that's why they're under so much attack regarding righteousness by faith—all other issues are just side issues. Righteousness by faith is the big issue with which the Adventist movement continually wrestles.

I think the Advent movement has had more ministers leave on this issue than on any other. I believe this is the beginning of the last-day shaking, and many Adventist members are now like sheep without a shepherd. They have either become so worldly that you can't distinguish between the church and the world, or they've gone to an opposite extreme because they're so fearful of doing the wrong thing. And in between is a large number of members just anxiously and desperately searching for light and understanding.

So we're living in interesting times.

CHAPTER NINE

"Having Been... We Shall Be"

Let's take another look now at Romans 5:1: "Therefore having been" (notice the tense) "having been justified" (an accomplished fact) . . . "having been justified, we have peace with God."

Peace with God is rooted, not in my circumstances, not in my spiritual growth, and certainly not in the fact that I'm not now doing some things I used to do. Peace with God—and I'm going to say it again—is not rooted in my circumstances. Circumstances can change! Maybe somebody reading this is about to file for bankruptcy, somebody else is about to file for divorce, or somebody has a child who is having a serious emotional problem. I mean, we all face things in life, don't we?

The bottom may have fallen out of your whole world, but the good news is that peace with God is not rooted in your circumstances. It's rooted in an accomplished fact, and that fact has everything to do with the death of Jesus Christ.

So the good news God entrusted to Seventh-day Adventists was given to them so that the errors associated with the Reformation could be set straight! This was quite frankly the main reason God raised up this movement.

And the beautiful message God gave the pioneers of the Advent movement was that salvation is both an accomplished fact and an ongoing process. It's both! And those two things are wrapped up in the death and resurrection of Jesus Christ!

How did God make sure the Advent movement didn't miss this? Calvinism missed it. What did God give those pioneers that guaranteed they wouldn't miss this particular truth?

It was the sanctuary. Because the sanctuary service was based on what happened in the courtyard—the established fact that a perfect lamb had been sacrificed. But then, the blood of the lamb was taken through the sanctuary. This sacrifice and ministering of the blood happened every day—an ongoing process. And on the Day of Atonement it was brought to conclusion.

The result of that ongoing process in our lives is—pull it out of Romans 5:1—peace. That's why people whose circumstances change dramatically don't have to lose their peace, because they know that what they have is not something they have deserved, earned, or contributed toward. It is something God has given them freely through His grace.

Notice the two verses that focus on this more clearly than others—verses 9 and 10:

"Much more then, having now been justified by His blood, we shall be saved from wrath through Him. For if when we were enemies we were reconciled to God through the death of His Son, much more, having been reconciled, we shall be saved by His life." (NKJV.)

The first clue we have here is that justification is associated with the blood of Jesus. But notice too the rest of verse 9: "we shall be saved."

"Having now been...we shall be saved." Are you seeing it? Don't miss it!

Having been, we shall be. We need to hear the language of Paul here. His tenses are so important.

"Having now been justified by His blood, we shall be saved from wrath through Him."

I hope you're seeing it: "Having been...shall be."

On now to the next verse: "For if when we were enemies we were reconciled to God through the death of His Son . . ."

Notice the parallel here: *justified by His blood* and *reconciled by His death*.

Now notice the rest of verse 10:

"Much more..."

And all of a sudden we start to hear that the "having been" is associated with what aspect of Jesus? His death. The "having been" is always associated with the death of Jesus.

But the "shall be" is always associated with His life—His resurrected life!

Please don't miss this—it's perhaps the single biggest theme in the writings of the Apostle Paul.

"Having been...we shall be."

"Having been this...we shall be this."

So why do so many people get into trouble in understanding the issues of righteousness by faith? Most people I'm relating to—what are they concerned about? The *having been*—or the *we shall be*?

Outwardly Focused

It's the *we shall be.* That is their concern.

"Oh, but you know, in my life I have things that are not going well. I'm not handling them very well. I'm still making mistakes. I'm still doing this—or that."

They're always focused outwardly, on their circumstances and their performance.

But if I'm hearing the Apostle Paul correctly, he's saying, "This (the "having been") precedes this (the "we shall be"). God is really saying, "If you'll just get out of the way long enough to see how gracious I *have been* to you through the death of Jesus—and then when you see it, embrace it and say, 'Thank You, God!'—that would open the door for all of *this* (what we can and shall be)."

And what prevents us from seeing this with gratitude? The reason we have such a challenge here is because we're still buying into the idea that "if I don't do the right thing, God isn't going to feel good toward me."

We're still making ourselves the means by which we receive the grace of God. And there's no freedom in that, because the natural human being, quite frankly, is not prone to doing right things all the time. You'll be robbed of the very thing you want, which is the presence of the Living Christ within you, who alone makes right-doing possible!

I'm going to write it again here: Jesus does not live in anybody who fails to appreciate what He's done in laying down His life for them. He doesn't do it. Because otherwise, He'd be indwelling people who were really not trusting and believing and rejoicing in the fact that they have a sacrificial, loving, and giving God—a God who has already justified them!

Savior and Lord

You see, when He justified us by His blood, Jesus was basically in what role? He was our Redeemer. But as He indwells us through the Spirit, giving us His resurrection life, the role of Jesus is to be the Lord of our lives, saving us *from* our sins. God never saves His people *in* their sins. Salvation is always deliverance *from* our sins.

God does constantly woo and draw and lure us to Himself. But there is a point when we see the cross, and we move into belief in Jesus as our Savior. Then we invite Him to come into our lives and indwell us. We call this being "born again."

Let me ask you now—who are the lucky recipients of God's free grace? What condition are people in—must they be in—in order to receive this grace? Scan through Romans 5, and you'll see. Let's list a few of the descriptions we find:

Helpless . . . ungodly . . . (verse 6)

And what was the benefit given to the "helpless" and the "ungodly"? The death of Jesus—His blood—was freely given to the helpless and the ungodly!

Other descriptions:

Sinners . . . all men . . . enemies . . . (verses 8, 12, 10)

And what benefit was given to these enemies? Reconciliation.

More descriptions:

Condemned . . . (verses 16, 18)

Now notice this carefully: this list we've been making, that includes the helpless, the ungodly, sinners, all men, enemies, and the condemned—is of those doomed to an *eternal death*. It's pretty serious.

But notice something else just as carefully. Can you see why sinful men and women are never in a position to feel that they can earn, deserve, or demonstrate to God their worthiness? God knows that! So He gave His own Son, whose perfect life was offered as a sacrifice, thus enabling God to declare righteous all of these people—the helpless, the ungodly, sinners, enemies, all men, the condemned. In God's reckoning *all* sinners have been declared perfectly righteous in His sight. Incredible!

God, in His infinite mercy, has accepted one Man in lieu of this whole world. And the moment you allow yourself to say, "Wow—that's incredible!" you are, in the words of Paul, in what condition? You are under grace!

You can spend every day for the rest of your life simply looking at the cross and saying, "I'm amazed! God has given me the most incredible evidence of His love! He's declared me righteous!" That's the Greek meaning of *justification*, you know—"declared righteous." So you can say, "He has reconciled me to Himself. And I've done nothing to deserve it—I couldn't!"

I have nothing to prove about myself to God. There is nothing to prove, nothing good, nothing deserving of commendation. What did Paul say of himself? "I am the chief of sinners." Yet that didn't prevent him from boldly working for God. It was his understanding of this that gave Paul the motivation to keep working for God despite the most horrendous opposition.

You could actually spend the rest of your life under grace—do you realize that? Because if you are not under grace, according to Paul, you are under law. And if you're under law, I've got news for you. You better be prepared to defend yourself before God. You better show Him that you have in fact—incredibly and miraculously—been able somehow to bring your life into perfect conformity with His perfect standard. And if you can demonstrate that, bully for you!

That's what it means to be under law. It means you believe that through your own attempts, maybe even generously giving God the credit for helping you, you can bring your life into conformity with God's impeccable standard. I wish you luck!

So the single biggest challenge any of us faces every day of our lives is to remain under grace. And the factor that makes that possible is that incredible little word: *belief.*

It's not by accident that John says in his epistle, "Whoever confesses that Jesus is the Son of God, God abides in him." 1 John 4:15. Think about that. Somebody who's confessing that Jesus is the Son of God is entering into belief every day of his or her life. The single biggest challenge we all face every day of our lives is to remain under grace by entering into belief. It's a powerful thing.

"Antichrist" is a word that means you're not entering into belief in Jesus—that you think you've found an alternative way to meet God's requirements.

All that God has done for us was done without our contribution. And what He has done covers every category of sinner.

A young homosexual came to my office one day. And he said, "I've got a big question—you probably can't answer it."

I said, "Go ahead."

"Is there grace for homosexuals in the Adventist church?" he asked.

"Well," I replied, "do you want the theoretical or the practical answer? Theoretically, there's much, but practically, I'm not sure I can assure you that you're going to find it in this congregation." But I said to him, "I tell you what—you can have that grace today if you qualify."

"Well," he answered, "how can I qualify?"

"You would need to convince me," I said, "that you are helpless, that you are ungodly..."

"Oh," he interjected, "that won't be too hard."

"... that you're a big sinner."

He said, "That's me."

"... that you're an enemy of God's, that you're feeling terribly guilty and condemned."

"I'm all of those things," he said.

"Well, then," I answered, "I've got news for you. The grace of God is yours!"

It's just not *effective* for anybody who thinks that they are apart from these things—that these words don't apply to them—like the Pharisees who stood proudly on the street corners, putting in their offerings publicly so people could see how righteous they were. That's the toughest thing for God to break through.

God's Grace Is for Everyone

By the way, this should be wonderfully heartening and encouraging to all of us, shouldn't it? Because there's no category, there's no sin, there's no depth you've fallen into which puts you outside the grace of God. Because God was in Jesus, reconciling you! 2 Corinthians 5:19. He wasn't asking you to do the impossible so He would feel better toward you. Knowing you could never do that, He gave His own Son!

Consider what God is offering to us! He has given us not just the privilege of being justified—as an established fact—but much more than that, He is offering us the privilege of receiving His life here and now! And that is salvation. Salvation happens when a person takes hold of the established fact, and opens up now for the life of Jesus to come into them. You have entered into salvation.

Often people ask me, "Are you saved?" I answer, "I have been saved, and I am in the process of being saved. I'm under the grace of God, and I praise Him for that. That's where I am."

Because salvation is an established fact, when we take hold of it by faith, the door opens for the very life of Jesus now to come upon us.

Made Righteous—and Declared Righteous

I hope that by now, you're seeing a clear distinction between being *made* righteous in contrast with being *declared* righteous. The meaning of justification is to be *declared* righteous.

I'm going to say it again: The only people I know who are being made righteous—who are growing up into holiness and maturity in Jesus—are those people who are daily appreciating that God has declared them to be righteous through the obedience of Jesus.

If sinners have the privilege of being made righteous, they can *believe* they will be made righteous. And they have this hope, based on the fact that the "obedience of the One" (Romans 5:19) not only enabled them to be declared righteous but to be made righteous. It's the "obedience of the One" that guarantees that they will be made righteous. What self-doubting and guilt trips believers can avoid every day of their lives, if they believe that through the "obedience of the One" they are guaranteed the privilege of becoming righteous! They won't have to feel lost or outside of grace every time they make a mistake.

You may even come to the place, as I did, where you can say, "I'm actually free to make a mistake! Because God knows I can't and don't change all that rapidly! I've got a thick head! I'm not complete overnight."

Because of grace, we don't have to spend our lives measuring how well we're doing, monitoring our behavior, worrying about our progress, and constantly asking, "Am I good enough?"

Have you ever heard someone say (perhaps it was you!), "I'll never be good enough"? You know, somebody actually wrote a book—an Adventist woman wrote a book called, *Never Good Enough*. And that is how far too many—even good Adventists—truly feel. But when you understand that God's full salvation includes not just being declared righteous but being made righteous as well, you will never even have to ask yourself the question, "Am I good enough?" Why? Because you are depending not on your own obedience and goodness—but in Paul's words, on the "obedience of the One."

What radical conclusion might we possibly come to at this moment about the obedience of Jesus? If it's only the "obedience of the One" that God accepts as the means by which we become righteous and are made righteous, then I'm just wondering if you are having the same radical thought at the moment as I am.

Here it is: "I'll never be the owner of the obedience—it will always be Jesus who owns it." None of it belongs to me or comes from me. It's all from Jesus.

This is a profound, remarkable breakthrough—to see that it's *His* obedience.

Now to some, this may be a radical thought, but I'm intending it to be so. The clear Bible truth is that the life Jesus lived was a perfectly obedient life. And that life—and Christ's death—has been accepted by God as the basis of my being declared and made righteous!

So I'm forced to the amazing conclusion that the life that I will live in the future *has already been lived* in the past, because it's the obedience of the One who has been accepted by God as my righteousness! And even the privilege of my being made righteous hinges on the life that *He* lived, not on the life that I will live! I am simply learning, by faith, to put on *His* life. I'm not just trying to do better with some additional help from Jesus—I'm putting on the life of perfect obedience that He has already lived!

That's radical! I hope now you're beginning to realize that putting on Christ's life is conditional upon the established fact of the cross.

The truth is that if that established fact is not in place in your life, and you are not daily coming to the cross, seeing there what God has done in the death of Jesus, and praising Him for it, you will probably find yourself in short supply of the Holy Spirit.

Because Seventh-day Adventists are not in the Pentecostal tradition. They don't just throw their hands into the air and say, "Fill me, Lord," and get filled.

The Spirit is in the ministry of bringing the life of Christ into believers! So our challenge is to remain in belief—to remain under grace—and to thank God for that grace every day of our lives!

"Hallelujah! God, You've declared me righteous! Thank You for the obedience of the One whom You have accepted totally and completely as me!"

This opens the door in our lives for the ongoing process—for the life of Jesus to come into us so we can grow into His likeness. And it's God in us from the beginning to the end, both "to will and to work for His good pleasure." Philippians 2:13.

Yes. Profound. Remarkable. Amazing. Radical, even.

And the basis of our hope.

CHAPTER TEN

The Most Important Daily Habit

I think I can say that through my many years of ministry, people who've come to me with serious lifestyle problems have shared, without exception, the same thing in common. They do not spend time with the established fact that "God was in Christ, reconciling the world unto Himself." 2 Corinthians 5:19. They do not see and appreciate that God has demonstrated His love in Christ and poured it out in the person of the Holy Spirit—that Jesus was the only human being to live a life totally obedient to God, by trusting in His Father.

Jesus is the only human being who ever overcame the devil. We were born drawn to the devil—He overcame the devil. In human flesh, He overcame temptation in every form. And the vast majority of people I know are defeated because they are trying to become Christ. They want to do what Christ did.

"I want to be strong enough so I can resist the devil at every step. I've got to overcome this sin. I'm going to be totally free of it."

Those kinds of statements all say the same thing. And what is it they say? They reveal that I'm buying into justification by works—

the assumption that grace can be purchased, earned, or deserved. If I've got the performance, I'll have the grace!

When you believe this way—and I too was there for years—you keep digging a hole deeper and deeper. You try harder, you cry out to God, and you beg Him to make you stronger and better.

But finally God opens your eyes and says, "You know, it's a question of belief. By the obedience of the One, many are made righteous. I am satisfied that one human being has already lived a life totally obedient to Me, and it's such a remarkable and perfect life that I'm willing to accept it in the place of the lives lived by *everyone!* The ungodly, the helpless, the sinners, even My enemies! The guilty, the condemned."

Jesus lived the life that I would have been expected to live. He's already lived my future life! So from now on I'm going to live by putting Him on every day. I'm going to have Jesus living, walking, talking, breathing, deciding, acting, and ministering through me!

I'm not planning to get better—to become more holy—by receiving regular injections of goodness from Jesus. Instead, I'm going to give Him the privilege of bringing into my life the very life He's already lived.

Let's return for a moment to Romans 5:1 and 2: "Therefore, having been justified by faith, we have peace with God through our Lord Jesus Christ, through whom also we have obtained our introduction by faith into this grace in which we stand; and we exult in hope of the glory of God."

What is this "hope of the glory of God"? Notice—it's the glory of *God.* "The hope of the glory of God" is that God will do with us what He's promised to do—and that is to *make* us righteous, not just *declare* us righteous.

You see, God is glorified when we permit Him to *make* us righteous, or in other words, when we put on the complete life that Jesus lived!

Notice this passage from John 17:4 and 5: "I glorified You on the earth, having accomplished the work which You have given

Me to do. Now, Father, glorify Me together with Yourself, with the glory which I had with You before the world was."

So Jesus' ministry was to glorify the Father. And how did He go about glorifying the Father? He did it by revealing the fullness of the Father in His own life.

So Jesus glorified the Father, and in turn, Jesus was to be glorified through His followers. And the purpose of Jesus being glorified in the lives of His followers was "so that the world may know that You sent Me, and loved them, even as You have loved Me." John 17:23.

The Bible Meaning of Glorification

God is ultimately glorified in the lives of His children as they reveal Christ. So the world around them sees Jesus in the lives of His followers, and the world then sees that God loves them too, and they are drawn to Him.

This is an incredible thing! This is the biblical meaning of glorification. It's too bad that we've often seen glorification reduced primarily to describing the time when we get new bodies, you know. Because glorification is actually a character issue.

With this brief look at John 17, let's go back now to Romans 5. This chapter is all about how gracious God has been to the human race. It's about how gracious God has been to you. It's about how gracious God has been to me, and to anybody who qualifies as one of the helpless, ungodly, sinners, enemies, guilty, or condemned.

While we were not in a position to offer God any reason for believing that we were deserving of anything, God gave His grace by sending His own Son, and gave us the privilege of justification, totally apart from ourselves. We were not involved. We did not contribute. In fact, we were in our lost and sinful condition when He gave us His grace.

God offered His own Son to live a godly life, to lay that life down, and then to be resurrected to make it available to anybody who truly believes that God could have been this generous!

And it's the biggest challenge of ministry to get people to forget their circumstances, their struggles, their failures, their successes—and to enable them to look objectively at the cross and say, "Hallelujah! Even in my ungodly condition, God loved me enough to lay down His life, to reconcile me, to justify me, by letting my death fall upon Jesus, who became sin for me so that I might have grace now available to me. Jesus lived a totally obedient life so that I might be made righteous, because He wanted to earn the right to offer me that very life.

And for 2,000 years that's just what Jesus has been offering His children. Yet sadly, comparatively few of His children have actually taken advantage of what He offers to them. Jesus wants us to have the fullness of what He is and what He lived. It's available. We can have His love. We can have His compassion. We can have His purity. We can have His fervor. We can have His self-sacrificing spirit. There's nothing we'll be denied.

And all He asks of you now is to remain under grace. In other words, to not slip back into thinking that something you have done earns His favor. What He gives you—what He does for you—is absolutely free, because you were incapable, you were ungodly, you were a sinner, and you couldn't do anything to accomplish your salvation. You had nothing to offer, so He says, "I've given it to you freely."

And it's encouraging to know that in response to God's gift, some do fall on their faces before Him and say, "Thank You! You must have loved me a great deal to ask Jesus to do all this for me—to look at me in my ungodly state, to declare me righteous, to take my death and my tendency to try proving that I'm not so bad, to take all those things upon Himself—so I can be set free to enjoy a relationship with Him and receive His life imparted to me daily through the Spirit.

To the Cross, Every Morning

If I can only get people to really see the cross, there's no limit to what God can do with them and in them. My burden is to get people into the serious habit of coming to the cross every morning of their lives.

Have you developed in your life the habit of coming to the cross every day of your life? Do you every day focus on the death of Jesus and claim for yourself *all* that is yours?

By the way, the world is sometimes much wiser than we are in these matters. They understand habit formation better than Christians do, I've decided. Because the world knows that it takes sixty consecutive repetitions for a habit to be established.

One time, to help someone establish the habit of morning worship, I called a fellow sixty mornings in a row, every morning at 7 a.m., and had worship with him over the telephone. About the fortieth morning, he said to me, "You know, you don't have to lead out anymore. I'm capable of doing this myself now."

"OK," I said, "you can lead out, but I'm still calling, because there are sixty days on the line here, and if we miss a day, we start again." That was the understanding. And he hung in there for sixty consecutive days!

What is your habit? Is it an established habit in your life to come to the cross every day and take hold of what you have through the death of Jesus? And what you have is totally free grace! You haven't contributed. You cannot do anything to change yourself inside. It is God loving you just as you are.

And the moment you come to the cross and acknowledge that God put all your sins, your imperfections, your condemnation on Jesus because He loved you, the Holy Spirit is immediately made available to your life for that day. You need never spend a single day of your life without the Holy Spirit indwelling you—without having the mind of Christ! What a blessing that is!

When you see how gracious God has been to you, there should be a point at which you can just open up your life and say to God, "I'm overwhelmed. I'm so undeserving. I know I have nothing to offer You, but I'm so grateful that You love me enough to let my death, my sin, fall on Jesus. And I want to claim and receive all that You have given and are offering me."

Friend, are you rejoicing in God's free salvation?

Have you thanked Him for that great gift?

And have you given up all—*ALL*—your efforts to earn or deserve it?

CHAPTER ELEVEN

Faith Statements

In this chapter, I want to talk about faith statements—what they are, and what they are not.

We need to be clear about what it means to enter into belief regarding the death of Jesus—and then be able to express that belief. And it really bothers me when I know we're not expressing our faith with clarity—that we're not really seeing what we have through the death of Jesus.

So I want to give you some examples of faith statements, because these are confessional statements. You know, confession, biblically, is not primarily spilling out all your wrongs. Confession, biblically, is testifying to what you have in Christ and praising the Father for it.

Faith statements deal with established facts. In other words, faith statements are based on what we know we already have, while we are helpless, ungodly, sinful, enemies, guilty, and condemned. These things are ours already. We can claim them!

And as we do, what door does it open? What miraculous,

dynamic door is opened when you confess that Jesus is the Son of God? Notice 1 John 4:15: "Whoever confesses that Jesus is the Son of God, God abides in him, and he in God."

Do you see here what happens when you confess your belief in the free gift God has given you in the person of Jesus Christ? Yes, you are indwelt. The Holy Spirit comes into your mind.

What a Faith Statement Is—and Is Not

Before we move into more discussion of this indwelling, however, I want to be sure we understand what it is to express faith in the established fact of what Jesus did for us at the cross.

Sometimes I almost wear myself hoarse just trying to get people to say it! Because, you see, they often have all these other thoughts in their minds, and some quickly launch into describing how well they are doing as God helps them to live better lives.

But such statements as these are not faith statements. They're good statements. They're not "offensive to God" statements. But they're not belief or faith statements, because faith is always rooted in the death and resurrection of Jesus Christ.

So you can actually look up and say, "Thank You, God, because this morning, through the death of Jesus, I praise You that You are looking at me as a righteous man."

That's a faith statement.

"Thank You, Father, that You are considering me today to be reconciled unto You through the death of Jesus."

That's a faith statement.

"Thank You, Father, that through the death of Jesus, I am no longer considered to be an enemy of Yours."

That's a faith statement.

"Thank You, Father, this morning, that through the obedience of the One, You are looking at me as if I had never sinned."

That's a faith statement.

If you have Christ abiding in you through the Spirit, then God is assuring you now that you are in Him and that nobody can take you out of His hand.

One time I was kneeling on the stone floor of a church in Latvia as a woman was praying in Russian. The woman spent twenty minutes giving herself to God and confessing every known sin she had in her whole life.

And I asked an interpreter, "What is she praying? My knees are giving out on me on this stone surface."

He said, "She's confessing every known sin in her life."

I said, "Hallelujah! We could be here for weeks!" You know?

Anyway, finally, after twenty or twenty-five minutes, she stopped praying and got up. This was a woman who'd had a demon problem for twenty years—never been free. She got up off her knees and threw her arms around my neck.

She said, "Oh, thank you! It's the first time in my life I've felt free."

And the Spirit of the Lord spoke to my mind and said, "Rebuke that woman."

"What?" I answered.

There were fifty young pastors around me that I was training as they were taking a seminary class. But God said again, "Rebuke that woman."

So I was having this argument in my mind with God. "Why?"

"Because," God said, "her prayer is not a prayer of faith. Because when you come to Me, you don't come offering Me something. You come to receive what I have given you."

At that moment, this issue became crystal clear in my mind, and I began to think of all the appeals we hear about, such as "Give yourself to God." We should be hearing many more appeals about how much God has given us—and to take hold of that by faith!

And I began to think, well, what am I actually offering God? Lucky God—look at what I am giving Him, you know? Notice this incredible body and mind I'm offering to God! Yet it's nothing compared to what God has already given me!

So from that moment I switched the focus of my entire ministry. And only on rare occasions will you ever hear me calling people to give themselves to God, because I'm far more concerned that they take hold of what God is giving to them.

It can be tempting to spend more of our time talking about our daily struggles—and how we apply Christ's salvation to our lives. And it's natural to be fascinated by that. But very few take the time to get the foundation in place—the established fact of what happened at the cross.

Now let me return to that church in Latvia and finish the story. It was an embarrassing situation for me, because I was training 200 pastors, and fifty of them had stayed behind and were watching my interaction with the woman who'd been praying. The interpreter had been telling me, "Ignore this woman. She's dangerous!"

Well, it's pretty embarrassing when you've got a woman sitting in the front pew waving at you. And finally she stood up and said, "Why are you ignoring me?" I said, "Ohhhh!"

So I allowed myself to minister to her, and she was really shocked.

"I've got a message for you from God," I told her.

"Oh," she said, "this is wonderful!" And she fell down and began raising her hands into the air."

I said, "Don't be too hasty. You haven't heard the message yet!"

"Well," she replied, "what is the message?"

"God wants me to rebuke you," I said. The blood drained out of her face.

"Why?" she responded. "I've just spent twenty-five minutes giving God every sin in my life!"

"Well," I answered, "that appears to be the problem, because when you come to God believing, you don't come offering Him something. That's the heathen way. You come to receive what God has given you. And you spent twenty-five minutes giving God yourself—yet you haven't once reached out and taken hold of what He's given you."

And by the way, this is symptomatic of many people. And if there's a shortage of the Holy Spirit in the life, I'm confident it's because we have not taken the step of confessing that Jesus Christ is the Son of God. It's that serious.

We urgently need to develop the habit of making faith statements when we come to God, because what did we just read in 1 John 4:15? If we do that, we will be indwelt by the Holy Spirit! Confess your faith in the death of Christ, and the living Christ will come into you! You will have Christ in your mind! Imagine what an advantage that is.

Now, if you don't have Christ in your mind, you'll be like so many other Christians. You'll be tempted, and you will desperately start crying out to God to make you stronger so you can withstand the temptation.

Seeing With a New Mind

But that is not the way to victory. That's the way to defeat. You can cry out for all you're worth, but in vain. But when you confess Jesus and He comes into your mind through the Holy Spirit, you immediately have the mind of Christ. You look at things with totally different eyes when you have the mind of Christ.

I know the first time it happened to me, I actually allowed myself to look at a beautiful young lady without any thoughts of lust, because instead of asking God to take away thoughts of lust, I said to Him, "I give you the privilege of coming into my mind."

And suddenly I looked at this girl that I had truthfully lusted after, and I looked at her and saw this beautiful creation that had come forth from God's hands—not an object of sexual desire but somebody beautiful who could glorify God. And, I thought, I should be praising God for His creation.

"Where did that thought come from?" I asked myself. It was not my accustomed thought.

And God said to me, "That's My thought. That's how I view beautiful young women who've come forth from My hand."

And suddenly I realized, "Oh, I've put the cart before the horse."

I had been coming to God with a carnal (unspiritual) mind, crying out for deliverance. My cry had been: "Make me stronger!"

I should have been coming to God with a Spirit-filled mind. Then I'd be thinking as God thinks. I want to tell you, when it comes to victory, this makes all the difference between success and failure.

And the privilege of having Christ in your mind through the Spirit hinges on whether you have permitted yourself to see and appreciate how much God has given you in the person of Jesus Christ.

You should be able to move into faith statements when you come to God each morning: "Thank You, Father."

What are you then going to say to the Father? Besides thanking Him, what else can you do? You could praise Him. You could sing praises to God. But your prayers are addressed to the Father. You are thanking and praising the Father for something that you have in Christ!

You have justification. He became sin for you!

This is how the Father sees you in Christ. "Thank You, Father, because in allowing Jesus to become sin for me, You now see my wretched, sinful self as being absolutely righteous in Your sight."

That's a faith statement.

I'm addressing the Father. I'm claiming what He's done in Christ. I'm allowing Him to see me as He says He sees me! And I'm acknowledging at the same time the truth about myself. I'm saying, "I'm a wretched, sinful person, yet You let Jesus become sin for me. And now You see me as sinless, righteous, and just!"

I try to express these thoughts to God every morning of my life. No matter how I feel, I want God to know my thoughts. "I am a wretched, sinful man, and I'm so grateful this morning, as I look at the cross, that You allowed Jesus to become sin for me, because now I have the assurance that in Your sight, for another day, I am as perfect as Jesus was."

That's a faith statement.

And you can do this concerning any of the blessings associated with the death of Jesus. And which category do all these blessings fit into? They are not part of an ongoing process in our lives. No, they are established facts. They have already taken place. They were ours when we least deserved them. We could do nothing about earning them. Yet despite our ungodliness and weakened state, God's grace was showered upon us!

So few people are truly grateful for the grace of God, it seems. Many professed Christians, including some members of the Seventh-day Adventist Church, have managed to develop ways of earning the favor of God or demonstrating somehow that they deserve it.

So—some will try to keep the Sabbath a little better. Others will practice righteousness by diet. They become a little more careful about the way they're eating.

Why not be free to enjoy God on the Sabbath? Instead of having to spend your whole life thinking, "Well, now, I've got to be sure I don't cross this little line." It's like the rabbi telling you that you can't ride outside the perimeter of the house, you know?

When we rest on the established facts—when we by faith accept what Jesus has accomplished for us on the cross—we can forever abandon our efforts to earn or deserve something that is, after all, already ours!

CHAPTER TWELVE

What a Relief It Is!

I'm the kind of person that can have a mountaintop experience, and the next day I can be in the valley. It's OK to acknowledge that to God about yourself, you know. That's how inconsistent we fragile human beings are in sin. That's what it's done to us! We actually begin to think the "yo-yo" experience is the normal experience. It's not!

So we're seeking to clarify our thinking about what it means to move into faith and to praise God for the gift of His Son on Calvary. It's the crux of everything. The whole sanctuary service began in the courtyard at the altar. It was the basis of everything else that happened!

After I had preached this very message in Australia one time, a man stood up and said, "Thank You, God, that I'm doing so well."

I looked at him in amazement! He gave the microphone back to the deacon, and I said, "Give it back to him again." The man was angry with this—this was someone I'd known for thirty years, you know? We went to school together.

And he said, "Well, I don't know what to say. Well, then," he continued, "OK, God, as I look around this church here, I want to praise You, because it's my money that built this church."

That's what he said the second time around. And I looked at him in even greater amazement. He tried four times, and still he couldn't acknowledge anything.

Finally, he said, "Well, I guess I don't know how to praise God."

"Well," I replied, "that could be a true statement."

He waited for me outside the door of the church. I knew he would. He was really angry and said, "You put me on the spot in there."

"Well," I answered, "you ain't seen nothing yet, because quite frankly—and I'm saying this kindly—you need to be put on the spot. If as a leader in this church, you can't stand up and praise God for what you've got in Jesus while leaving yourself out of the picture, you've got a problem!"

He still hasn't succeeded in expressing a true faith statement. I mean, every time I'm there, he tests me again. He's determined to win.

We should praise God for all the blessings of life, but if we're not entering into belief, we are robbing ourselves of the indwelling of the Holy Spirit, and we're just becoming better educated little devils.

You're reading the words of somebody here, remember, who for twenty years prayed that self-defeating prayer, "God, make me strong enough. I want to do this for you."

And God finally said, "But, look, I've already done it for you! Open your eyes and take hold of what I have done in human flesh! Believe in Jesus—you don't have to *be* Jesus!"

Trying in Vain to Be Super-Human

That's what He told me. And I thought, "What a relief!" I was indeed trying to be Jesus. I wanted to be the perfect overcomer. I wanted to have a pure, righteous life. I hated the fact that I still had some habits in my life that were not to the glory of God.

But I was going about it the wrong way. I was wanting God to make this person super-human. But there's only one human being who ever was good enough!

And God in His infinite mercy has accepted that One in my place! Amazing! How could He do that?

When I finally saw it, I just fell on my knees and said, "Forgive me for twenty years in the wilderness of trying to get stronger."

And God said, "Well, you had good motives, but it didn't work, did it?"

"No," I admitted, "it didn't work! I'm deeper in the hole than ever!"

And that was the first moment I saw some light!

I was like Luther. Yet why did I have to repeat Luther's experience? I should have been content to read of his discovery and believe it—that "the just shall live" not by struggle, not by begging God to make them superhuman, but that "the just shall live by faith" alone!

And that faith is in the Lord Jesus Christ.

You will even know how God feels about your fellow workers, because it will be God's mind in you looking at them. You'll know the very moment when you should be nurturing, when to be a little bolder, when to be supportive. You'll know precisely when, because it will be Jesus in you who looks at others lovingly, wanting to draw them to Himself.

Remember 1 John 4:15? "Whoever confesses that Jesus is the Son of God, God abides in him, and he in God."

Now I don't mind telling you that if you make a Biblical confession—a statement of faith—you can expect to be anointed by the Holy Spirit. And remember, that could carry a risk because of the results it brings to your lifestyle, to your relationships, to everything else about you.

A statement of faith is based on established facts—and those facts are found in the Word of God. The Bible story of the centurion's slave shows that you're in faith when your requests are based on the Word. Luke 7:1-10. If God has said it, you are free to take hold of it as boldly as you like and claim it for yourself.

And no, this is not arrogance. It's called "faith" to believe that since God said it, I believe it, and that settles it. The reason it's not arrogance is because it's contrary to the natural human heart. The natural human heart wants to do things itself and is even happy to call on God to make it stronger to be able to do them.

But faith is based on humility and surrender. I acknowledge my own uselessness, my sinfulness, my helplessness—and I need what God has given and is offering me through Jesus Christ. That is faith. You can be as bold as you like.

Anyone in the Bible who saw God didn't stand up and say, "Oh, thank You. I'm not a worm."

You know what they did? They said, "Woe is me! I'm a man of unclean lips, because my eyes have seen the glory of the Lord. I've seen how holy God is and how sinful I am by contrast." See Isaiah 6:1-5.

That doesn't mean that God doesn't place value on us. Don't get that wrong. But Christianity is the opposite of "pop psychology." In Christianity you begin—well, it's like in Alcoholics Anonymous, where one begins, "I am an alcoholic."

And in what I call "Sinners Anonymous," you begin by saying, "I am a man, or a woman, of unclean lips. There's nothing good in me."

But this doesn't mean that I'm without hope. That's a different matter altogether. Yet unless we acknowledge the truth of what sin has done to us, we never seem to get beyond first base in having an assurance of salvation.

That's why I emphasize and repeat that salvation is an established fact as well as an ongoing process. And part of the established fact is the realization of our utter sinfulness.

How did God feel about the world in Noah's day? How was it described? "Then the Lord saw that the wickedness of man was great on the earth, and that every intent of the thoughts of his heart was only evil continually." Genesis 6:5.

"Every intent!" And what did Jesus teach? "As it was in the days of Noah," every thought in man's mind was evil.

This is what sin has done, and the beauty of Christianity is that despite the acknowledgment of our utter helplessness and sinfulness, we are not without hope; because God has seen value in us to the point that He's sacrificed His own Son, knowing what sin had done to us.

In other words, God is not offended when we come boldly. He wants us to come boldly, because of what He's done in Jesus Christ.

So let's track down a few of these faith statements.

"Thank You."

"Praise You."

"Sing Your praises."

BENEFITS OF THE DEATH OF JESUS

You can do it however you want to, because through the death of Jesus Christ:

"I've been justified—declared righteous." Romans 5:9.

"I was reconciled to God." Romans 5:10.

"God has demonstrated His love toward me." Romans 5:8; 1 John 3:16.

"God has made peace, reconciling all things—including me—to Himself." Colossians 1:20

"I was redeemed—bought back—and forgiven." 1 Peter 1:18, 19; Revelation 5:9; Ephesians 1:7.

"I was crucified with Christ." Romans 6:5-7; Galatians 2:20.

"He became sin for me, and died as me." 2 Corinthians 5:14, 21; Isaiah 53:4-7.

"My sin has been put (or taken) away." Hebrews 9:26, John 1:29.

"I have been released from my sins." Revelation 1:5.

"I can consider myself to be dead to sin." Romans 6:11.

"I have no second death in my future, because He's already died that death for me." Hebrews 2:9.

"I have been freed from my enemy, Satan—he's been defeated—he is powerless over me." Hebrews 2:14.

"I am free from the fear of death, from slavery to sin and the devil." Hebrews 2:15.

"I am…" what else?

"I have been perfected forever, even while I am in process of being sanctified by Christ!" Hebrews 10:14.

"I was healed." 1 Peter 2:24.

"I'm no longer condemned." Romans 8:1.

Why not?

Because my condemnation fell on Him. Romans 8:1-3; 1 Peter 2:24.

All of these things, I have, despite the fact that I am helpless, sinful, and wicked.

All these blessings, I have, and they're all mine on the basis of the death of Jesus! These are established facts, and I can simply say, "Thank You, Father. There's no second death, no hellfire, in my future. I want to praise You for that today, because Jesus has already died my second death."

That's a faith statement.

"Thank You, Father, because even though I have felt as if I were on death row, bound by sin, I am not condemned in Your sight, because You graciously allowed my condemnation to fall on Jesus."

Amazing! *Condemned,* by the way, is the same word as *judged.* My judgment fell on Jesus. It killed Him. That's why Jesus taught that a true believer "does not come into judgment" (John 5:24)—because He's already experienced it!

"Thank You, Father, that I don't have to spend today in ignorance of Your love, because You have demonstrated Your love toward me in sacrifcing Your Son to die in my stead, and I want to rejoice in that love today. Thank You."

That's a faith statement.

"That was the demonstration of Your love. Thank You, Father."

My favorite faith statement always comes back to justification: "Thank You, Father, that despite awareness of my own sinfulness and humanity today, as I look at the cross, I'm just in awe of the fact that You see me just as perfectly righteous as Jesus, because though He knew no sin, He permitted Himself to be made sin on my behalf (2 Corinthians 5:21) and to suffer the death that I deserve (Hebrews 2:9). Thank You, Father."

That's a faith statement. And the moment you say it—the moment you confess—the Holy Spirit brings the life of Christ into you. How do we know that the faith statement above is true?

Because Jesus was sent to death, and death is the wages of sin (Romans 6:23), not of righteousness. Jesus—even though He never sinned personally—became sin. That's why the Father turned His face away. Not because He saw His own Son, but because He saw you and me hanging there. Jesus took my sin on Himself. The Father "caused the iniquity of us all to fall on Him!" Isaiah 53:6

If you ever let Him become fully you, what a moment that is! One day I actually allowed Jesus to die with everything on Him that I was. I mean everything. I thought, "Hallelujah!" Jesus took even my weakest, darkest, most horrible thoughts, actions, and attitudes on Himself. And it killed Him! It was a faith step on His part, as it is a faith step on our part to take hold of that and believe it.

We know it cost Him His life! Righteous men don't die like that—not the second death. He died *the second death*—the death of a guilty, forsaken sinner. What an act of faith it was for Him to do that! He had to believe that His Father would raise Him again.

Contemplate the following beautiful quote from Ellen White in *The Desire of Ages,* page 25:

"Christ was treated as we deserve, that we might be treated as He deserves. He was condemned for our sins, in which He had no share, that we might be justified by His righteousness, in which we had no share. He suffered the death which was ours, that we might receive the life which was His."

How is your faith right now, my reading friend? I want to encourage you to write out a faith statement of your own. It shouldn't have anything to do with your struggles in life, with how well you're doing, or how well you're not doing. It should instead bring your focus to the death of Jesus.

In your faith statement, you'll praise God for the death of Jesus, because anything in Scripture that relates to the death of Jesus, you may claim as yours. And you simply want to praise God for being so gracious and generous.

Let me give you one more example of a faith statement:

"I'm thanking You this morning, Father, because through the obedience of one Man Jesus Christ, who was obedient unto death, You see me as totally obedient to Him. Thank You, Father! Because when I look in the mirror, that's not what I see, but I'm praising You, because that's what You see—and it gives me the courage to press on in Jesus Christ."

So take a moment now and write out your own faith statement on the next page. Because when you do, it will unlock the Holy Spirit in a very special way, and you can expect interesting things to begin happening within you!

I also want to encourage you to find a friend or family member and verbalize your faith statement—"If you confess with your mouth Jesus as Lord, and believe in your heart that God raised Him from the dead, you will be saved; for with the heart a person believes, resulting in righteousness, and with the mouth he confesses, resulting in salvation." Romans 10:9, 10.

MY FAITH STATEMENT:

Thank you Father for allowing Jesus to die for my sins, and you only see me through Jesus.

CHAPTER THIRTEEN

"Much More"

We are declared righteous through Christ's death, and then as the Spirit comes into our lives, we are, in fact, made righteous. That's that balance we've been looking at, so praise the Lord for that.

Some of you may still be sliding a little toward the ongoing experience side, but I want to be sure that we continue to praise God for what we have through the death of Jesus—an already established fact. This, in turn, opens the door for the magnificence of the Holy Spirit's work in our lives. God is good, isn't He?

If you take hold of Christ's death by faith—and all that God has given you—you'll be a peaceful person. You won't be punishing yourself. You won't be on a perfectionistic trip. You won't be measuring your performance every day to see if you still have the favor of God or not. You will be focused on the cross of Calvary. And all those things will be lifted from you, and you will now be free to enter into Christ's life!

That's why the promise is, "If you confess, He will abide within you!" And this is an ongoing *process.* I find it absolutely fascinating that so many Christians see a sinner come to Christ and then expect instant maturity. They've obviously never reared a child.

The most important part of baptismal preparation is not a set of doctrines—it's the knowledge of Jesus Christ. After a while you're going to discover that all the doctrines of the Seventh-day Aventist Church were intended to be Christ-centered, too. They were not to be a set of teachings to support a church. They were to reveal much to us about the character of God and what He did in Christ. That's what the doctrines are.

Doctrines can be life-giving when they're presented in a Christ-centered way. I mean, we're never called just to defend a set of doctrines. That's not our reason for existence. We're called to lead sinners to life! And if there are sinners in the community, they should be coming to Seventh-day Adventist churches seeking freedom and life and victory—and the ability to live without being enslaved for the rest of their lives.

At this point, I'd like to ask you to stop reading this book. Yes, you heard me right! For a moment, at least. Long enough so you can take some time to find your own Bible and read through Romans, chapter 6.

....

Did you finish Romans 6?

Now then, notice the use of the word *consider* in verse 11. Is it "faith" or "feeling" when you "consider" something? It's a "faith" experience, isn't it?

"Consider it," "choose to believe it." What word does the King James Version use there? *Reckon.* Yes, that great old word, *reckon.* Or "count." OK, we've got several options here: "reckon," "count," "consider," or you could say, "choose to believe."

When you choose to believe, you can claim all the benefits of Christ's death. It's the first step in our day as we come to the cross. We're looking at practical steps now. And the first habit we want you to get into every day is the habit of confessing your belief in and gratitude for the death of Jesus.

There can be appropriate feelings, by the way, that accompany a statement of faith. God gives good, healthy feelings to people who express their faith.

The more we share these things, the more they become a part of us. You're not free because somehow, you've improved your life. You're free because Jesus lived not an "improved" life but a perfect one! You know?

God had to lift the guilt that was crushing the human race! Even though we may have been addicted to sin, we still felt guilty about it. So Jesus had to submit to being treated as we deserved to be treated—as absolutely sinful. He had to suffer death. And only the death of a righteous Man could ever have atoned for the sins of the whole world.

Yes, it was our sin that brought death to Jesus. At Pentecost when Peter stood up and preached that powerful sermon and 3,000 were converted, he said to the Jews who were present, "You killed Jesus." That was exactly what He preached! He called a spade a spade, and they were convicted and repented! See Acts 2:36-41.

We all have the capacity to fall away from keeping this as the focus of our daily lives. But God is gracious, and the interesting thing is that He doesn't plunge us back under condemnation. We, however, put ourselves back there quickly enough!

But God doesn't put us back under condemnation, because it was not lifted from us in the first place because we were consistent in living as we should. It was lifted from us because God loved us enough to let Jesus experience it in our stead. That is grace. That's what grace is all about.

The Only Basis for Our Assurance

What God has given us is the basis of our assurance. I hope you all see this. This is our *only* basis of assurance. It's the basis of our assurance because all the benefits of the cross have been given to us, not on the basis of our human performance—they are given to us on the basis of Christ's divine-human performance! So even if we do slip back—which we've all done—and we get so busy that we can't always keep this awareness in place in our daily lives, we're not plunged back into condemnation and guilt. Because we were never declared righteous in the first place because we were doing so well—but rather, because Jesus did so well!

That's why what God gives us is the basis of our assurance. And you can avoid the yo-yo experience if that one factor is in place in your daily life. You can start to have a consistent experience of belief and assurance.

But you will soon realize, that God is offering you "much more" (see Romans 5:10). Those two words should leap from the page of your Bible and flash as in neon lights.

"Much more."

Much more than what? Let's read the whole verse: "For if while we were enemies we were reconciled to God through the death of His Son, much more, having been reconciled, we shall be saved by His life."

The Good News is that even as we were God's enemies, we were reconciled to Him through the death of Jesus. Yet…there's "much more"!

Please don't miss this! What God is offering you is not just the privilege of being free from a death sentence—a pretty marvelous privilege, no one could deny! This would be like being let out of death row!

But God wants you to know that He has "much more" in store for you! That's why Protestantism began to fall back when it stopped at the cross. Because the cross was the pathway to "much more"!

And it's not enough just to go through life knowing that I'm forgiven, that I'm pardoned, that God is looking at me as if I'm perfect. God is offering me "much more"!

How much more? What does it say? *We shall be saved by His life!* God wants you to know that He's not just giving you forgiveness—He's also offering you restoration. In other words, salvation is not a passive experience. It's a dynamic experience! If you enter into salvation, you are entering into life! And I hope you've seen from what you've read so far, that the way to life is through Jesus' death! You cannot get to life without going first through the death of Jesus.

Jesus taught this Himself. "Unless a grain of wheat falls into the earth and dies, it remains alone; but if it dies, it bears much fruit." John 12:24.

The way to life is through death!

This is where some incomplete Christian teaching has not served many of us well. We've been taught that God loved us and forgave us, but then left us with habits of sin that somehow we haven't always been able to put behind us! And this gets discouraging!

It led me to cry out to God one day, "This system doesn't work!"

Yet God has been so patient with me.

But God wants you to know that "much more" than what you have through the death of Jesus, you're going to be given restoration through His life! You are now free to receive the life of Christ!

And I hope you're utterly clear that the life of Christ cannot be imparted to anybody who's not partaking by faith in His death! Because you'd still be under guilt and condemnation, yet wanting life at the same time.

You'd end up in this weird duality—this double-mindedness—where you sit in church and hear the sermons and can even talk about the second coming of Jesus, and then you go out and fall back into the same old paths of sin over and over again.

That was not God's plan for us.

CHAPTER FOURTEEN

Baptism, Death, and Life

Do you know what baptism is really all about? It's reaching a point where you're willing to acknowledge publicly that it was your sin that Jesus took on Himself, and your death that He was dying. Jesus was a pure and righteous Man, and that's what we acknowledge at baptism.

We acknowledge not only that in His death, we died—but that also we now live in His resurrection life. This is what we've been saying all along in these pages: that our salvation is both an accomplished fact and an ongoing process. So baptism is a time for declaring your absolute identification with the death and the resurrection of Jesus.

It would be too bad if it ever simply became a time when you agreed to 28 doctrines and joined a church. What a tragedy that would be! If only we were as concerned to lead people to the understanding of the death and the resurrection of Jesus as we sometimes seem to be that they get all the doctrines straight. Those things would take care of themselves, because if you have truly come to understand salvation, then by the time you're baptized into Christ, you have received the mind of Christ, and you're open to anything else that He wants you to know and to believe. It's easy to put the cart before the horse.

I hope you're keeping your Bible open next to you as you read this book. Right now, I'd like you to turn to 2 Corinthians 5:21: "He made Him who knew no sin to be sin on our behalf, so that we might become the righteousness of God in Him."

Why did Jesus die and become sin in the sight of His Father? So we might become righteous!

So many people have no idea what it means to enter into salvation. They think it means, "Well, I'm finally going to get to go to heaven and live on and on and on . . ." Life forever is certainly included as part of our salvation, but salvation isn't something we must wait for—something that is far off in the future. No, salvation means to enter now into the life of Christ!

One of the first New Testament uses of the word salvation was in Matthew 1:21: "You shall call His name Jesus, for He will save His people from their sins."

"From their sins." Yet so many seem to believe that the verse reads: "in their sins." I'm serious. A lot of people apparently believe that.

Set Free

Salvation means to be set free from sin! That's what it means to be saved!

But if someone says to you, "Are you saved?" what are they thinking? You're going to heaven. You're going to live on forever and ever and ever—almost regardless of what you do.

Yet Jesus died so that we might become "the righteousness of God in Him."

The whole purpose of His death was to open the door for us to be restored back into righteousness—the righteousness sin has taken from us! That is the meaning of salvation. You enter into life, and that life is in the Son. So "he who has the Son, has the life." (See 1 John 5:11 and 12.)

Baptism, Death, and Life • 95

If you have Christ in you, you have His life! You'll no longer be a slave to sin. God will restore you into righteousness. That's His promise! The only problem is, it's not an instant thing—it's an ongoing process in our lives.

I don't know how many people are boggled when they begin to realize that salvation is not some floating-around privilege in heaven. It's actually a very real, earthly experience. Eternal life is a present reality, because that life is in the Son! He who has the Son, therefore, has this life! That's why we ought to spend our lives seeking Christ! We need not be trying to improve ourselves, because the only way to improve oneself is to have Christ. There's no other way. There's no other power, or name, given among men, whereby we might be saved. See Acts 4:12. And saved means transformed, restored to righteousness, given the kind of life that can actually endure living.

Imagine if God took us all to heaven right now, where absolute unselfishness reigns—where pure love is the order of the day. Now, God is gracious. The thief on the cross did not have time, so he'll have the privilege of growing up in heaven. God knows that this is a process that takes a lifetime for most of us. And even then we look at ourselves and realize how short of His glory we still are.

One of the most astounding things I've ever read in the Bible is a statement in Ephesians. I keep going back to it and reminding myself—this is what God is promising us. In Ephesians, chapter 3 is one of the most beautiful passages in the New Testament—about the height and depth and length and breadth of God's love.

I'm looking at Ephesians 3, verses 17 to 19. What an incredible passage this is: "So that Christ may dwell in your hearts through faith; and that you, being rooted and grounded in love, may be able to comprehend with all the saints what is the breadth and length and height and depth, and to know the love of Christ which surpasses knowledge, that you may be filled up to all the fullness of God."

I nearly fainted when I first read that. I said, "No way."

God is offering me the fullness. I have to confess to you, I have difficulty handling a few drops of God's holiness when He reveals it to me. And He's offering me the fullness—the fullness!

In other words, you can be as loving as God is, because it is actually God loving through you.

You can be as forgiving as God is. It is a miracle, because it's the One who said, "Father, forgive them; for they do not know what they are doing" (Luke 23:34), who's forgiving through you!

Peter said it so beautifully: We "become partakers of the divine nature." 2 Peter 1:4.

It's God in us!

I'm going to tell you again that there is no power on this entire earth that can bring about that kind of change to a human heart. You can sit through all the self-help seminars, go to all the counseling, try everything that this world has to offer, but it will not change your heart. But allow Jesus to dwell in your heart by faith, through the Holy Spirit, and in one moment, you can have the mind of God.

You will think the highest thoughts. You'll have the deepest feelings. You'll have the most profound love. You'll experience the most incredible confession, repentance, and forgiveness. And you'll extend it all to others, because Christ will be in you.

And when Christ is in you, the Bible says you can consider yourself "to be dead to sin." Romans 6:11. That's the toughest thing in the world to choose to believe when the evidence points to the contrary. Because, whether we like it or not, we do feel sin within us pulling us a certain way. Can we all say that this is a true statement?

The Pull of Sin Within

I believe you're going to feel the pull of sin within you until the Lord comes, and it's totally unrealistic to expect that you will not feel your propensity to sin. In fact, the Word is that those who come into the spiritual realm and are born again of the Spirit feel the pull of sin much more intensely than people who are carnal by nature.

Sin never used to bother me at all. People who are born of the Spirit and are walking in the spiritual life sense and feel the presence of sin within them much more strongly than people who are not in the spiritual life.

That's why, when you look into the Law of God, you feel condemned, because you see the holiness of God, and it shows your own sinfulness.

No, sin never used to bother me. I used to enjoy it! But then the Law came, and I looked into it, and as Paul says, "I died." Romans 7:9.

Paul actually says the Law made his sin even more sinful. It magnified it. It showed him how sinful he really was by contrasting it with the holiness of God. See verses 10-13.

So if you're expecting never to feel the propensity and the pull of sin within you, I've got news for you. You're on the wrong path. You're going to feel it more intensely than ever.

Finally one day, you may cry out with the apostle.

"It's not me!" he said. "It's sin which dwells within me. It's not me God—it's sin within me." See verses 17 and 20.

And God understands that. It's one of the reasons He gave Jesus the exact flesh we have. After 4,000 years of sin had weakened humanity, Jesus then took on the body of a human being. Think about that.

That's why Jesus felt what we feel. It's so encouraging to me to know that Jesus had a true human body, yet was without sin. When I realized that, it was the first time in my life that I began to consider that sin is actually not something physical.

There is a point in our spiritual growth, the Bible says, where we can consider ourselves to be dead to sin. But apparently that doesn't mean that we don't feel the presence of sin within us! We're going to discover what it does mean.

So now let's look at Romans 6:6: "Knowing this, that our old self was crucified with Him, in order that our body of sin might be done away with, so that we would no longer be slaves to sin."

Our old self, crucified with Christ. And that brings up a question. At what point in the Christian life does this become a reality? At what point can we actually claim this?

Paul gives us the answer in this chapter, and it must precede the knowing this of verse 6:

"Or do you not know that all of us who have been baptized into Christ Jesus have been baptized into His death? Therefore we have been buried with Him through baptism into death, so that as Christ was raised from the dead through the glory of the Father, so we too might walk in newness of life. For if we have become united with Him in the likeness of His death, certainly we shall also be in the likeness of His resurrection." Verses 3-5.

So our understanding of baptism can point us to an answer. Because at baptism, some people may perhaps be expecting *their own* death—the death of their old nature. But baptism is the time when you are baptized into *Christ's* death. And if you're being baptized into His death, then what is the one thing you should have an understanding of above anything else?

The cross! The atonement! The significance of His death!

Because by the time of your baptism, you are at a point where you've become convicted regarding the death of Jesus and its incredible benefit to you! That is the point when you should go forward into baptism, because you are willing now to be baptized into His death.

And again, it's through the acceptance of His death that we are opened to receive His life. But often it's a real task to get people to focus on Christ's death, leave themselves out of the picture, and see how good God has been in Christ—so that now God can indwell them and bring about all that they've really wanted from the beginning: a holy and pure life to the glory of God.

Because God's not going to varnish you. He's not going to improve what you are. He's going to come in and recreate you and restore you back into His image! And I have news for you. It can be a painful process, yet a very joyful experience.

And it's all ours, by faith!

CHAPTER FIFTEEN

Joining the Body of Christ

What is the root of our peace?

We've already found it in Romans 5:1: "Therefore, having been justified by faith, we have peace with God through our Lord Jesus Christ."

Peace doesn't depend on my being truthful with God. Rather, I have peace because of the established fact of "having been justified," so I'm now able to be truthful, open, and honest. It's not the other way around.

We don't convince God, by being truthful, to become generous with us. It's *because* God is generous with us in the condition we're in—this hopeless, helpless, ungodly condition—that we're enabled to be truthful.

And Christ is offering to come in, through the Spirit, and bring changes from the inside out. He's not offering improved performance. He's offering to actually come in and indwell us.

One thing I love about God is His ability to incarnate Himself in human flesh. Whenever He visits earth, He always takes on human flesh.

Jesus came to earth—He took on human flesh. The Holy Spirit came to earth—He indwelt human flesh. This is God's specialty. He specializes in incarnation.

You can actually become a partaker of the divine nature. You can have God in you. And there's no power equal to that anywhere in the universe—having divinity within you. It is a transforming, life-changing, overpowering, overcoming thing to have God in you, because you're taking into you the very One who, in human flesh, overcame sin and the devil. You're putting Him on!

Now, when believers enter truly into faith, they are then filled with a desire to declare this. Baptism was always intended to be a public thing, because at that moment, when you're willing to declare it publicly, you are saying, "I'm now ready to connect with the body of Christ and become a functioning part of it."

So the entrance into the body of Christ has always been through baptism, and God's response to baptism has always been the anointing of the Spirit.

I was in Australia a while back, and one of my nephews—an elder in one of the Seventh-day Adventist churches there—came up to me and said, "Look, I've got this young couple, just in their early twenties." And he said, "I've been studying with them, and they wish to be baptized. I've asked the pastor, and he's given me permission to do the baptizing."

This was exciting for my nephew, because he hadn't done any baptizing up to this point. But because he'd worked with this couple, the pastor told him to go ahead and do the baptizing.

"But," he said to me, "they don't want to join the church."

So he asked, "What would you do? Would you baptize them?"

"No. I wouldn't," I replied. "It's interesting that I'm saying this to you," I added, "because there was a time in my experience when I probably would have. But since then, I've grown to understand that baptism is the point in our lives when we feel ready to connect to others who have also sensed that they died with Christ at His cross and want to become a functioning part of His Church."

So I took my nephew through some of the great chapters in Scripture. For example, we looked at Acts 19, where Paul came to Ephesus and said, "Did you receive the Holy Spirit when you believed?"

And they said, "No. We haven't even heard of the Holy Spirit."

Paul then asked, "Well, into what were you baptized?"

Paul knew that at baptism, they should have received the Holy Spirit, which is an anointing for ministry within a functioning spiritual body. So he went ahead and rebaptized them. He laid hands on them—and they were commissioned for ministry. Gifts fell upon them. They were activated for service.

So I said to my nephew, "If you baptize people, and they're not becoming a part of the spiritual body, they're going to sit in the pews. They're going to die. They'll wither up. They won't be active in ministry.

No one person has ministry—the whole body is in ministry. The hand can't say, "I'm in ministry." But the hand can say, "I'm part of a body that's in ministry to the glory of God. It's the body of Christ." 1 Corinthians 12.

I took him through all this, yet he hadn't told me—and this was Friday night—that he was planning to baptize them the next day. I wish he'd told me that, but he never mentioned this little fact.

Anyway, he went to this couple the next morning and told them he wouldn't baptize them until he'd had further study with them. And on the following Tuesday night, when they'd gone through the study, they said, "Well, why would we *not* want to be a part of the spiritual body?" So they joined the body at the time of their baptism. It was a beautiful experience, and my nephew too grew a great deal through it.

Baptism is the time when you seek entrance into the body of Christ, but the transition from the established fact into the ongoing process happens the moment you enter into belief.

But remember, you really can't grow alone. You can't become more loving alone. That's why God brings us into the body, because our preparation for ministry involves growth as a functioning part of a body. And as we learn to need one another and appreciate the uniqueness and the different gifts in one another, we grow in our usefulness to God.

God is very wise in these matters. So in a sense, true growth happens once we become an effective part of the body. But the Spirit, of course, has been at work in our lives leading us to belief—and even as we enter into belief.

Nonetheless, something solid begins to happen the moment we take a stand, and we declare it and come into the body of Christ—and the Spirit anoints us. That's when real growth, from my experience, takes place in people's lives. I've seen people muddle along for years and finally take a stand, and then overnight they're unleashed. It's exciting.

CHAPTER SIXTEEN

A Radical Inner Change

What we have through the death of Jesus is an established fact. It's ours—and we did nothing to earn it. It has been given to us as an absolute free gift. So many incredible blessings are ours through the death of Jesus: forgiveness, justification, reconciliation, the stripping of our enemy of all his power (we only have to mention the name of Jesus, and the devil flees from us!), and our redemption.

All of these things and more are ours. We can claim all of these benefits.

But the word *salvation* is always tied together with reception of the life of Christ, because salvation is dynamic. As we've noted already many times—it is both an established fact and an ongoing process.

I'm going to say it again—the life of Christ is given only to those of us who, by faith, take hold of God's love gift to them in the sacrificial offering of His Son.

As we take hold of that by faith, God promises to abide in us! You can believe that. You can go and act like a person who has

God in you. But I want to warn you: It's dangerous to let God be in you. It's much safer to look at Him on the cross and say, "Yes, He must have loved me. Look what He's done."

But if you're going to let Him live in you, that's an intimate thing. Because the presence of the living God in you challenges your thinking, your feelings, your actions, your attitudes. Nothing is left untouched when you let the living God in you.

So I say to people, "Count the cost before you let God live in you, because He will not leave you as He found you."

He will refine, He will restore, He will replace, He will change. He will sculpt you. He will mold you. He'll even permit trials and tribulations to come into your life just to get you to the point where He can fully reveal Himself in you. That's how gracious He is—and you'll kick and scream! At least you will if you're anything like me. Two times in my life I've actually had to say to God, "Back off, please! I can't handle this stress anymore. You promised that You wouldn't allow us to be tempted more than we can endure [see 1 Corinthians 10:13], and I'm putting You on notice right now that I cannot endure, not even another hour. You have to reduce this pressure on me if You wish to have me as a loving and obedient son."

I put God on serious notice, because I said, "I'm in danger. I just can't handle it anymore."

Giving God Permission

There are limits, apparently, that all of us have. I have a high pain threshold myself, so to reach a point where I actually said to God, "I can't stand it!" meant I was at an incredibly high level of pain.

And God is so gracious, He backed off and turned the fire down, and things settled down. I was able to get my breath again and go on.

"Thank You for doing this for me," I told God. "It's not that I'm doubting or anything—I just couldn't handle this stress any longer."

God's very gracious like that. He's very understanding, but I gave Him permission to do whatever was necessary to round off the rough edges in my life.

At that time, He actually said to me, "Are you sure you know what you're doing, giving Me this kind of permission?"

"Yes!" I responded. "I really want those rough edges to be rounded off. I want the areas of weakness in my life to be eradicated."

He said, "Ohhhh-kay."

And He turned up the heat. I mean, I felt as if I were being singed. I could feel the flames devouring me. Finally, I just said, "Stop it, please!"

"Well," He said, "you're the one who gave Me permission."

"I know," I replied, "but I'm withdrawing it for the moment."

Now I'm getting back to a point again where I'm starting to give Him more and more permission. But He's so good, He'll give you a breather if you want and need it—a time when you can just get your breath and reevaluate and move forward.

I have found God very understanding in these matters, but it's a risk to let Him in.

I pray a "crisis prayer" on behalf of others quite frequently, but I say to God, "Look, I'd like You to really bring crisis into the life of this person, but I'm going to trust You with the level of the crisis, because You know what they need better than I do. All I know is that they're not really rejoicing in You and Your grace at the moment, and I'd like to see that."

I've even given God permission to bring crisis into the lives of all my children, for example, just so they could deepen their relationship with Him and that He could strengthen His hold on them.

One of my children actually called me up one day and begged me to stop praying. I said, "OK, I'll give it a break."

But God was gracious. He brought crisis into the lives of all my children, and little by little, I've seen Him strengthening His hold on them. And if ever I reach a point of concern with one of them, I pray that prayer again.

God is much more interested in the growth of our children than we are. Because He wants the privilege of having them with Him throughout eternity. And He knows, much better than we appear to do what it means to live in the presence of a holy God.

Wasn't it the sons of Aaron who, while serving in the temple as priests, didn't use the proper kind of incense and fire in coming before God? And they were consumed immediately! Leviticus 10:1, 2. And Uzzah, with the best of intentions, rushed over to hold the ark as it was falling off a cart—and was destroyed instantly. 2 Samuel 6:3-7.

You can't touch holiness with unholy hands! God was trying to teach His people this. Look what happened at Mount Sinai. God gave strict instructions when Moses was up on the mountain: "Wash your garments. Prepare your lives. You're going to be standing in the presence of the holy God. Don't touch the mountain! Don't even let your animals go onto the mountain. It's holy ground! On the mountain is the presence of God." See Exodus 19.

And we are going to be living in the presence of God. Yet most of us—if you're anything like me—are too casual about standing in the presence of God.

Finally, it hit me one day, God is not planning to take the seed of sin and rebellion back into His kingdom, and if it's in me, I'm not going to be there. And that wouldn't be because He doesn't love me. It would be an evidence that I refused Him permission to root sin and selfishness out of me, because of how painful that is.

And yes, it *is* painful, because we've lived with it our whole lives. That seed of rebellion is in us from birth, and God wants permission to root it out. He won't force you, but He will use circumstances to help make it happen. And any pain that brings will only be because He loves you enough that He does not want to spend eternity without you!

God is fully intelligent when it comes to salvation. He knows what it cost Him personally to atone for sin. And He also knows that anyone who embraces the sacrifice of Jesus is actually giving God permission now to make them fit to live with Him.

You've got your ticket to eternity with God, but now He wants to give you the fitness to enjoy what that ticket represents—the privilege of living in the presence of God.

It's a wonderful experience to be under grace every day of your life. You have the presence of the Holy Spirit living within you. You are able to claim all the blessings of what Christ has done *for* you—and what He now wants to do *in* you, through His Spirit.

And it's a wonderful experience to make the public faith statement of baptism. Baptism is the believer's way of saying to God, "I truly believe that the death of Jesus was actually my death to sin taking place in Him. I'm prepared to accept that it was my sin, not His, that killed Him. It was my death that He died, and I'm so grateful, God, that You allowed Him to bear that instead of me."

And by the way, baptism is to be renewed every day. How? Through the daily anointing of the Holy Spirit. That is actually a rebaptism every day, because Jesus taught us from His own example that baptism was always intended to be by water *and* the Spirit. You only need to go into the water once, but you need the anointing of the Spirit every day of your life, which is confirmation of the fact that you have died with Christ and been resurrected with Him. This is actually a form of rebaptism every day.

Outrageous Claims

And according to Paul, you are now in a position—and these are daily things now—to make some seemingly outrageous claims on God, and they're all by faith.

Let's look now at Romans 6:6-11: "Knowing this, that our old self was crucified with Him, in order that our body of sin might be done away with, so that we would no longer be slaves to sin; for he who has died is freed from sin. Now if we have died with Christ, we believe that we shall also live with Him, knowing that Christ, having been raised from the dead, is never to die again; death no longer is master over Him. For the death that He died, He died to sin once for all; but the life that He lives, He lives to God. Even so consider yourselves to be dead to sin, but alive to God in Christ Jesus."

This is such a significant passage. What we read here is now to become a part of your daily experience. You've come to the cross. You have confessed your belief in the death of Jesus. You have claimed the privilege of being justified—declared righteous, forgiven, reconciled—all those beautiful benefits that God has given you through the death of Jesus.

Now—and make sure you're reading and understanding this passage clearly—go back and look again at verse 8: "If we have died with Christ, we believe that we shall also live with Him."

It's the reception of the Holy Spirit into our lives that makes this possible. So now you can claim verse 11 for yourself every day: "Consider yourselves to be dead to sin, but alive to God in Christ Jesus."

Faith and Feelings

This is the faith step you take after you've been to the cross and you've thanked God for how generous He's been through the death of Jesus. You are now privileged—and notice now that this is where Paul himself goes here—to consider yourself to be dead to sin. It has nothing to do with how you're feeling. You may actually be feeling seriously tempted. You may actually feel something within you being drawn out after sin. This isn't feelings—it's a faith step. You consider yourself to be dead to sin.

I certainly thank God for this myself. Having looked at the death of Jesus and praised God for that, I then take this step and say, "Thank You, God, because today I consider myself to be dead to sin—and I also consider myself to be alive unto God. I'm Your child today. And as I leave home, what do I need? What do I need to be able to function as Your child?"

"Dead to sin and alive unto God," what am I going to need for this new day? I am going to need the Holy Spirit. And even though God has moved upon me, I like to reinforce this with God every day—that as a child of God who's no longer a slave to sin but now instead a child of the heavenly God, I need the indwelling of the Holy Spirit in order to function and live through another day.

I'd like to encourage you now to think of a Bible promise—or promises—that you could lay hold of to make sure that you're giving God permission for His Spirit to come into your mind at this moment. Because you're a child of God, you wouldn't dare leave home without the Spirit of the living God in your mind. And don't restrict yourself to the book of Romans, even though that's where we've been focusing.

For example, when I've asked my seminar students to find such a Bible promise, here are some of the ones they have found:

John 14:16: "I will ask the Father, and He will give you another Helper, that He may be with you forever." And that Helper, of course, is the Holy Spirit.

Psalm 51:10, KJV: "Create in me a clean heart, O God; and renew a right spirit within me."

Ezekiel 11:19: "And I will give them one heart, and put a new spirit within them; and I will take the heart of stone out of their flesh and give them a heart of flesh."

Philippians 2:5, KJV: "Let this mind be in you which was also in Christ Jesus." Of course, this is another way of asking for the Spirit, because the Spirit is the One who brings Christ into us.

As you think about this, you'll find your own promises of the Holy Spirit. And it's wonderful to get into the habit of claiming such promises each new day.

Remember the story of Jesus' encounter with Nicodemus? In John 3:3, Jesus told him: "Unless one is born again he cannot see the kingdom of God."

This certainly confirms a great truth we've noticed continually throughout these pages—that salvation is both an established fact and an ongoing process. For if salvation was just an established fact through the death of Jesus, and it all stopped there—an idea which much of Christianity buys into—you'd be forgiven, you'd be justified, you'd be reconciled, you'd have all those blessings, but you'd *still be a slave to sin!*

Jesus died—He became sin for us—in order that we might be made the righteousness of God in Him. And that's the "born again" experience. This incredible verse in John is telling us that if you're going to be in God's kingdom, you need to have guilt lifted from you *PLUS* give God the privilege now of remaking you, because salvation is a dynamic process in our lives.

By the way, included in the Good News is the assurance that if you're cut off before you reach the fullness of maturity, you will have the privilege of continuing to grow in the kingdom. The thief on the cross—how much of the "ongoing process" did he have time to experience? He didn't have a chance for that, but it didn't deprive him of what the death of Jesus guaranteed him. Had he lived on, he would have been given the Spirit and grown up in many ways into Christ. This is so important to know and realize and believe.

You can trust God with the ending of your life, you know. You don't ever have to live in fear of that, because in Christ you are perfect at each step of the way. Hebrews 10:14. Just as the flower that's opening up is perfect at each step. The reason this is true is because your perfection is in Him, not in you.

Now let me share something very important. When you receive the Spirit of God, He comes into your mind. This is the only part of the human body with which the Holy Spirit communicates directly.

Otherwise, we'd be into the "holy flesh" doctrine, which actually afflicted the early Advent movement a little. People started believing that the Spirit could come into other parts of the body. Yes, a very strange development. But it's the mind that is renewed.

And here's this beautiful statement from Ellen White in the article "Genuine Conversion," from the *Review and Herald,* July 7, 1904:

"The leaven of truth [a reference to the Spirit] works secretly, silently, steadily, to transform the soul. The natural inclinations are softened and subdued. New thoughts, new feelings, new motives, are implanted."

There is a lot of confusion over what we get "new." But here it is clearly spelled out. When we enter into our new life in Jesus, we receive a new mind. The new life is then lived according to that new mind. The one thing God cannot give us instantly is character. We act upon the new thoughts, the new feelings, and the new motives. That's the meaning of being born again. It's your mind being transformed.

"Let this mind be in you which was also in Christ Jesus." Philippians 2:5, KJV.

"Be transformed by the renewing of your mind, so that you may prove what the will of God is." Romans 12:2.

It took me years to recognize that with a new mind, the will of God is now inside me!

And when that is true, I no longer have to struggle to do God's will. I don't have to do His will because I have to—but because now, *Christ in me wants to!*

CHAPTER SEVENTEEN

The Mind of Christ

The mind of Christ in you brings the will of God into *your* mind. Ellen White said it so beautifully in *The Desire of Ages,* page 668:

> "All true obedience comes from the heart. It was heart work with Christ. And if we consent, He will so identify Himself with our thoughts and aims, so blend our hearts and minds into conformity to His will, that when obeying Him we shall be but carrying out our own impulses."

It's one of the highest privileges of a human being in sinful flesh—probably the highest—to receive the mind of Christ! This is God incarnate in you, but when He comes in, He doesn't do everything for you. He doesn't take every little step that you need to take.

What He does do is to change the most important part of your being, which up until then has been enslaved by sin. You weren't even capable, really, of doing anything differently, because *your* mind was in control. But now that mind has received new thoughts and new feelings.

I've known people who have really had difficulty in having new feelings toward somebody—to the point they couldn't even forgive. But with the mind of Christ in you, you will actually feel differently. no matter what anybody has done to you.

We've talked earlier about baptism. Let me say that there's nothing miraculous about baptism. If you want to see it as "miraculous," perhaps you should be a Catholic!

"But as many as received him," John wrote, "to them gave he power to become the sons of God, even to them that believe on his name." John 1:12, KJV.

Not to "as many as were baptized," but to as many as believed and received. You don't enter into belief at baptism—belief precedes baptism. But by the time you've reached the point of baptism, you are ready now to act upon your belief and connect yourself with the spiritual body of Christ. And you are prepared to declare your belief publicly and are now willing to be put to work and to function in the capacity God has ordained for you.

And you'll never know that special capacity or area unless you tie into the spiritual body. Then you'll know. At baptism, we publicly demonstrate our conviction. That's when we do it. But it's a conviction that could have been in us for some time.

So I'm not limiting the significance of baptism. Not at all. But the understanding and the belief factor will already have been present. You're just acting upon it at baptism, that's all. It's already a reality in your life. But don't underestimate what happens when you connect yourself with the body. That's when growth really starts to take place within believers.

So when you enter into this new life of being indwelt by the Spirit, what are you getting that's new?

New thoughts, new feelings, and new motives.

Now let me share here a statement that is perhaps the most profound thing I've ever read about the meaning of the new birth.

"A new standard of character is set up,—the life of Christ." Ellen White, "Genuine Conversion," *Review and Herald,* July 7, 1904.

When you receive the mind of Christ, you are now measured

by the life of Christ. There's a new measure—a new standard—in your life. You have now become subject to the law of love. It's in you. That's why these things don't apply to people who are not yet born again. That's why in Scripture, by the way, the term *wicked* applies to people who claim to be born again, but don't show the fruit of it. In the New Testament the term *wicked* is never used of the heathen. At the human level it's only ever used of *professed believers* who do not really have a living connection with Christ. (For examples of this, see Matthew 13:49, 50; 1 Corinthians 5:13.)

So there's a new standard set up in your life. And notice what then happens:

"The mind is changed" Ellen White, "Genuine Conversion," *Review and Herald,* July 7, 1904.

If you're anything like me, you need to have that change in your mind every single day. Because if I have one day without inviting God into my mind by faith, I find myself reverting back to my old natural thinking processes. Do you find the same thing true for you? And before long I could be totally back into my own ways of thinking and doing.

Carnal and Spiritual

There's a fine line between being carnal and being spiritual. When a carnal person surrenders to Jesus Christ and acknowledges his or her hopelessness and helplessness to change, then in one moment of time, God graciously infuses Himself into the human mind, and we have again a miracle on earth. We have a spiritual person in a fleshly body—a great miracle.

Everything hinges on the mind, because in the mind is located the will. And everything, I mean *everything,* hinges from now on, on the right action of the will. We're getting now into the real "practics" of what happens when you're born again.

So God is not indwelling you and saying, "OK, I'm now going to cause you to do this and this. You'll be like a little puppet." Not at all. God is renewing the control center of your whole being. And as He comes into your mind, you will be empowered with new thoughts. You'll have new feelings. You'll be able to forgive the most unforgivable.

One time in California I saw the most unforgivable forgiven, when a man stood up in a seminar. He said, "I can't hide it any longer."

"What?" I asked.

"I have to make a statement," he replied. "I'm under intense conviction, and I want to announce something to all of you—and to you, Pastor. I know that at the moment I make this statement you will have to call the police, and I'll probably spend the next twenty years in prison. But I can't live with myself any longer. I have to have this new mind. I'm not at peace."

A truly dramatic moment—and right in the middle of a seminar.

So this man stood up publicly and confessed that he had been sexually abusing the daughter of a couple who were sitting in the seminar. Now, I nearly fell off the planet. It's probably the single most dramatic moment I've seen in a seminar. And he confessed it with weeping and with tears. I've forgotten how old the girl was—perhaps twelve or thirteen.

"And I'm sorry to announce," he continued—and then identified the couple in the seminar, "it's your daughter."

The parents were thrown into the most incredible consternation. I kept quiet. God told me to zip it up, "Say nothing."

"I consider," he went on—and I can still hear his words now, "I consider myself to be the most wretched, miserable specimen of humanity. It wouldn't surprise me if you could never bring yourselves to forgive me. I would understand. I know I'm going to be punished. By law, you will have to call the police."

"Yes," I agreed. "We will."

"I just can't live with this another day," he continued. "I'm not looking to excuse myself. I came from an abused family myself, but that's no excuse. There's no blame on this girl. I assume the full responsibility here."

Then, turning to the parents, he asked, "Could you find it in your hearts to forgive me?"

And of course, everyone was holding their breath and looking at this couple who were clinging to each other. They got up out of their seats—this husband and wife—and came forward. I don't think I've seen a greater demonstration of love and forgiveness, and I actually said to myself at the time, "Could I have done what they did?" I have a daughter, too, you know. Could I have done what they did?

The parents came and knelt down with this man and put their arms around his neck and forgave him! There was much weeping and repentance and a whole lot of forgiveness flowing at that particular moment.

The man was converted through this experience. He's still in prison but is apparently an incredible witness there, from what I'm hearing about him. He was actually converted in that dramatic seminar moment, because two people had the grace of God in them to forgive what most of us would consider to be the unforgivable.

Later, I asked the parents, "How could you do that?"

"We have been forgiven so much by God," they answered. "How could we hold back forgiveness from him? And now," they added, "we have to deal with our daughter's rehabilitation."

So I said to them, "I want to make a prophecy here—that because of the attitude of you two, your daughter is going to be totally healed of this. She's going to put this behind her, deal with it, and have a normal life. That's my prediction, because she will see in her own parents the kind of love and forgiveness that will melt her own heart."

And sure enough, I met this girl again recently. I mean, she was praising God! A beautiful girl. You'd be proud to introduce her to your son, you know?

And I said to myself, "Wow!"

I looked at this girl and could see her wholesomeness and

vitality. And she stood up and gave a testimony in a meeting I was conducting. It just about brought tears to everybody's eyes, as she told how, seeing in her own parents such love and forgiveness, she was enabled to embrace the love and forgiveness of God herself. Of course, she had made some mistakes herself, and she accepted that.

And again, I thought, "Wow!"

Maybe it's our own attitudes that at times rob kids of healing and the courage to go forward despite terrible things that can happen in their lives. If you are a parent, I don't know how you were (or are) in rearing your children. I was so paranoid that not one of my children spent a night away from home the whole time they were growing up. I mean, not even one night!

So, my heart was bleeding for this couple. Yet out of it has come the most profound healing. And what was this gentle, humble couple demonstrating? The mind of Christ.

"Oh," they said, "yes, we're grieving, and we're hurting badly for the damage that's been done to our daughter, but that doesn't give us the privilege of condemning this man."

And there, I actually saw in action the mind of Christ. I thought too of Jesus, when Mary Magdalene came to Him—and of how gracious He was to her. He even let her wash His feet and dry them with her hair. How forgiving and enabling that must have been to her—to know that Jesus was not treating her as some prostitute or woman of ill repute! Instead, He demonstrated the fact that she could even minister to Him. Jesus teaches us so much about forgiveness, doesn't He? He let even the greatest sinners minister to Him, because His heart of love was drawing them.

Once you put on the mind of Christ, you realize how far from Him most of us have fallen. Because we just don't offer unconditional forgiveness to some types of sin today. We don't do it.

I was preaching the Sabbath sermon at the North New Zealand Conference. About 5,000 people were sitting in a big tent. In one area of the tent, a young man was sitting. An area around him about twenty feet in any direction was vacant, because the word had gone out that he had AIDS. This was in the early days of AIDS when there was a lot of confusion about what really caused AIDS. And here's this kid—he couldn't have been more than 21—sitting there with a big empty circle around him.

I was preaching on the prodigal son (Luke 15:11-32), I remember, and God said to me, "OK, you've got an opportunity here."

So I left the pulpit, walked down into the tent, sat next to this young man, put my arm around him, and had a prayer with him. I think that did more than all the sermonizing I could have done. They still talk about it in New Zealand.

And I said to the people, "You know, I was compelled to do this, because God has forgiven me so much. How can I now sit in judgment on a young man whom I know nothing about—knowing nothing of the factors and forces that may have led him to this point? All I know is that he needs the grace of God at this moment."

And then I asked, "Is it possible that some of us have become the older brother?"

It was a marvelous illustration God gave me—especially as I was preaching on the prodigal son.

"Are some of us here the older brother today?" I asked. "Are we offended because a young man is finding grace, despite the waywardness of his life? Why would we be offended by that? We should be rejoicing! The older brother in the parable was offended because the father was putting on a feast for his younger brother. It offended him! He didn't think his brother deserved a feast!"

Great Sin—Great Grace

And those beautiful words of Scripture came through to me: "Where sin abounded, grace did much more abound." Romans 5:20, KJV. You'll never see greater grace than where there is greater sin.

So again now, what are you receiving when you receive the

new life in Jesus—His mind in you? New thoughts, new feelings, new motives. The mind is changed, but—and here's the interesting part of the statement we've been looking at—"The faculties are aroused to action in new lines." That's speaking of the faculties of the mind. Ellen White, "Genuine Conversion," *Review and Herald*, July 7, 1904.

Consider again what I have that's new: "new thoughts, new feelings, new motives." In other words, that's the change that has come into my mind. But the faculties of my mind are also aroused to action in new lines.

What are the faculties of our minds?

Reason, the will, all the senses, choice (that's the will), emotions, appetite, sexual fulfillment—all of these things are faculties of our minds. Every part of our being is controlled through the various faculties in our minds.

Now notice what Ellen White is *not* saying. She's not saying that the faculties are changed. She's saying they are "aroused to action in new lines."

This is very important to notice. For example, I mentioned sexual fulfillment—sexual desire—as a faculty of the mind. And I know young men who've come to me, saying, "I have this desire that arises within me."

And I say, "Well, praise God, that's the way He made you. You should be worried if you weren't feeling it, but what you *do* with it will determine whether you glorify God or spend your life just seeking self-fulfillment."

So when we receive the mind of Christ, that faculty is now aroused to action in new lines. And what's going to make it possible for that particular faculty to act now in a new and different way?

Having the mind of Christ, which means that now, I'm going to be looking at each faculty of my mind—whether it be appetite, reason, will, sexuality—differently than before. I mentioned earlier that when, for the first time I looked at a young lady without lusting, I thought, "What an original thought that is!"

Because, bear in mind, I came out of the world. I wasn't raised in the church. And that's the way we looked at girls. But here was a new thought. It wasn't until years later that I realized that this thought had come from the Spirit of God—that there is indeed another way of looking at girls.

For each one of these faculties, we've been operating with a certain set of guidelines in our mind, but as the Spirit of God comes into our mind, we start thinking of how they could be used differently to the glory of God.

So, those thoughts were not with me previously, but they're now with me, because God has come into my human mind and given me a new way of looking at something that had potential for good but had been used for evil.

Think of the implications of this concept in working with young people. We could go around saying to them, "That's wrong, and you shouldn't be doing this, and you shouldn't be doing that." But perhaps instead we should be targeting the mind, to lead our youth to have the mind of Christ so they can see all the attributes of their being as something with potential to glorify God.

So with the mind of Christ in us, this is what's new. This is what is now possible. New thoughts and ideas are in your mind, and it's this new mind that's going to make carrying them out possible. And what will the end result be?

THE MEANING OF SANCTIFICATION

Listen to the end of our statement: "Man is not endowed with new faculties…"

Did you see that? Unlike what most people think, "Man is not endowed with new faculties, but the faculties he has are sanctified." Ellen White, "Genuine Conversion," *Review and Herald,* July 7, 1904.

This is the meaning of sanctification. It takes place in the faculties of the human mind. The faculties are sanctified. Not renewed—sanctified.

And what you now need to do is to start acting upon that new thought, that new feeling, that new motive—to act upon it. And as you do, it seems to open the way for the Holy Spirit to strengthen within you the desire to remain inside those new lines instead of the old lines.

Habit Formation

But what we have failed to recognize, I think, for a long time, is habit formation. Some people, for example, have never established the habit of coming to the cross.

So here now is the Holy Spirit prompting me. Maybe it's concerning how I use my eyes. And the Spirit is prompting me now to act in new lines. If I make the choice to yield to that and to act upon it, I will be strengthened then to make the same choice the next time.

But the next time that I'm tempted to use my eyes in the old way, what must I do again? I need to come back into belief again. I need to acknowledge my inability to change myself. I need to ask God for the mind of Christ.

I had an experience recently in California, where a woman came up to me in the middle of the seminar. Speaking for herself and her husband, she asked, "Could we have lunch with you today?"

"Sure." I said. I'd known this couple for several years. So the three of us were sitting outside in the sunshine, and she said to me, "I can't forgive my husband. I don't want to go into detail of what it is, but I just can't bring myself to forgive him. I hate myself for this, but I will not forgive him. I can't do it."

He was sitting there, listening to this. So I said to her, "Well, would you like to forgive him in the next two minutes?"

"It's not in me!" she assured me.

"That wasn't my question," I told her. "I asked you whether you would like to forgive him in the next two minutes."

She looked at me and asked, "Do you think I could?"

"You're still not answering my question," I persisted. "Would you like to forgive him in the next two minutes?"

"Well, yes!" she replied.

"Thank you!" I said, "OK, repeat after me the prayer that I'm about to pray."

So we bowed our heads together. We were sitting at this table outside the church, and I said to her, "I'm going to pray as you, and I want you to pray every word I pray."

"God, I'm a mess. I profess to be a Christian, and I can't even forgive. I'm just so hopeless. I'm helpless! I can't change myself. I've tried! But I do believe today, by faith, that in Your sight I am justified. You are not looking at me as a big sinner. You are looking at me as a big saint, because all my sin has fallen on Jesus."

She repeated every word.

"And I just want to praise You for being so generous to me. And now, create in me a clean heart. I give you permission at this very moment to come into my mind through the Holy Spirit—to bring the mind of Christ into me. And I promise You that whatever thought comes into my mind after this, I will act upon it."

She hesitated on that, so I repeated it.

"Whatever thought comes into my mind when we've stopped praying, I will act upon it."

And she finally said it.

So I ended with, "Thank You. Amen"

She opened her eyes. She looked at her husband, and the woman who'd come to church unable to forgive her husband—well, I'm sure you *know* what happened! She reached out, and she just put her arms around his neck.

"Honey," she said to him, "how could I have been so stupid? Please forgive me." And she added, "I forgive you."

And then they said to me, "Look, do you mind if we go off on our own?" The two of them walked away hand in hand. They came back an hour later and were as happy as two people could be.

She came up to me and said, "That was incredible!"

"No," I said, "that was God! You did the one thing that Christians frequently forget to do. They spend their time complaining that they can't act, and they punish themselves, and beat themselves up. It's far better to move into belief, come back to the cross, praise God for what you've got in Jesus Christ, and give God permission to come into your mind!"

She had so much forgiveness flooding out of her that she kept asking her husband to forgive her.

"I thought you were supposed to forgive him!" I said.

"No," she replied, "my attitude's been so bad—he needs to forgive me!"

She totally turned around. I said, "That's the mind of Christ. He doesn't seek to justify Himself. He simply seeks reconciliation and unification and forgiveness and for love to come in."

Surrender—Not Struggle

Why do we struggle, when we ought to be surrendering? Why don't we simply surrender and invite Christ's mind to come into us? We'd have all His love, His joy, His peace, His forgiveness—all this would be ours.

We don't do it for one simple reason—and notice this carefully—we don't do it, because *we have not established the habit of doing it.*

Most of us—when we're under pressure, when we're stretched, when we're tempted, when we're facing situations beyond the capacity of our regular human natures (especially if we've moved into the spiritual realm)—most of us don't think of submitting our mind to Christ, to be renewed and to have His mind. We don't think of coming back to the cross and renewing our belief and confidence in what He's given us through His death.

We don't do these things for the simple reason that we have never established the habit of doing it. We would much rather kick and scream and yell and hold our old attitudes until they nearly kill us. Then, in desperation, we come seeking some help. We do not establish the habit of putting on Christ, so that divinity, blended with humanity, puts us now in possession of new thoughts!

That was a new thought to this wife! She almost seemed to hate her husband. Yet suddenly—and I was fascinated…it took about ten seconds after we opened our eyes—she looked at him, and I saw it on her face.

"Ahh-haa," I thought. "God's done what God does! He's given her a new thought! She loves her husband. She should forgive him! There's a new thought."

Then God gave her the new thought that maybe she should ask for forgiveness. That was the last thing on her mind. It was a new thought! Because she surrendered her will to God and gave Him permission to transform her mind, God's ideas came through.

How many difficulties in churches could be resolved just so quickly! I had two women in a seminar in Ohio who got into a fight in the middle of the seminar and started pulling each other's hair! I just stood there in absolute amazement watching this hair-raising experience.

So I dismissed the seminar. "You may as well all go outside," I said. "There's no grace in here, you know?"

I sat down with these two women. "You know, let's …"

"I'm not going to talk!" one of the two interrupted. "I'm not going to forgive her! Da-da-da-da-da!"

But the other woman said, "Yes, please share with me. I'm not happy with what I'm doing."

So one woman surrendered her mind, and she looked at the other woman and said, "You know, I'm sorry we've had this misunderstanding, and for my share in it. I seek your forgiveness."

The other woman looked at her. I'll never forget the moment. The other woman looked at her and said, "I will never forgive you as long as I live."

And I said to myself, "OK, the sheep and the goats. Both in sin. But one was willing and confessed and repented. The other woman piously and self-righteously refused to let go of her hatred."

I'll never forget those words, "I will never forgive you."

As it happened, we were holding the seminar in the home of the woman who said that. So I said to her, "This is our last seminar here, because I can't afford to be running seminars in a house where you will never forgive. You could have the mind of Christ that she has received and be as forgiving as that woman is."

But she couldn't do it. Very sad—but there are many like that. Many.

Victory is in surrender, not in fighting.

And surrender brings what we most need: the mind of Christ.

CHAPTER EIGHTEEN

New Spiritual Habits

Once we are in belief, we can give God permission to come into our minds—to give us His mind—and then God does what He's so good at doing. He can turn our thinking around in an instant.

It's when we persist in our own determined way, in our own strength, and with our own ideas——when we refuse to give God access to our minds—that we hurt ourselves the most. And it does make it more challenging for God to penetrate the walls we build around ourselves.

The Spirit's withdrawal from people is a very gradual thing, but we are actually the ones who lose the capacity to keep hearing the Spirit. We need to be objective in measuring ourselves by the Word, because certain things, we don't need to debate as to whether they are right or wrong. They are clearly addressed in the Word. I run into more and more people who are looking for a way around God's Word. They don't want to do what God says is most pleasing to Him.

Alright, something significant is about to emerge here. Two things are going to happen to you, if you get your new spiritual habits in place. The first thing is that you're going to lose the desire for—the attraction of—the old ways. And one day you're going to wake up and say, "It just struck me—that doesn't appeal to me anymore."

It will be so quiet and subconscious that you'll wonder when on earth it happened that you no longer have an appetite for that particular habit. But, it's gone from you.

The second thing that will happen is, you will begin to develop a love that will motivate you to do by nature the things that the new habit has now formed within you. In other words, you've cultivated a different response to the stimulus that previously triggered something within you. Now you have trained yourself, by the grace of God within you, to have a different response to that same trigger. All things become new.

Brain Pathways

And the reason this is a challenge for us is, as you all know, that in the brain are these little pathways. This is physiological. We know this. These *boutons* are set up in our brains, and the consistent development of wrong habits in our lives establishes actual patterns in our brain pathways. And when we are born again, they are not changed. So you can have a new mind with these old pathways still in there. And these pathways are habitual responses to things that trigger us. We call them stimuli.

I know I used to be triggered by posters. I used to go to X-rated movies, and they'd have these posters there. And if I would walk past the cinema and see that poster, it would trigger my old pathways, and I would go in.

And then I became a Christian. I thought, "Oh, well—that won't bother me anymore. I'm new."

So I deliberately walked past that old cinema I used to go to. And I saw that poster, and guess what? Whoop—I went in! I couldn't believe it! I sat through an entire X-rated movie with my eyes shut, praying that God would give me the strength to get up and leave that place. Nobody had ever explained to me that, when you become born again, the old pathways are still there! You can still be triggered. You can still be tripped up. You have to develop a *new* pathway. Now *that* is a big lesson for all of us to learn.

I also had a struggle with dancing. I came from a big drinking, dancing, partying family. And I went dancing every Friday night for as long as I can remember in my youth and adolescence. Every Friday night I was at the dance hall. Then a little lady came into our home, and we started having Bible studies. And one day she taught us about the Sabbath. Suddenly, it hit me. "Oh, no! Friday night. She said that's the Sabbath! Friday night."

And I began to think about my habit. I was already being convicted to leave the world, but I had *so many* worldly habits in my life.

Anyway, I used to take a train to night school. And I would come back about 8 o'clock at night, and I would exit the train and walk out through the gates. I could either turn left, or right, or I could go straight ahead. There were three different ways of going home. It was about half a mile away.

But on Friday night I was in the habit of always turning left, because that took me past the dance hall. Anyway, I was sitting in the train going to night school one particular Friday, and in the providence of God He had a young Methodist preacher sitting next to me on the train. I was telling this preacher what a struggle I was having to leave the world and to change my habits, and he took me into Romans 6, of all places—pulled out a Bible—and this is the verse he read to me. Romans 6:16: "Do you not know that when you present yourselves to someone as slaves for obedience, you are slaves of the one whom you obey, either of sin resulting in death, or of obedience resulting in righteousness?"

This is when I first came to grips with habit formation.

"The choice is yours," he said. "If you have God's Spirit in your mind, you can now make a conscious choice."

"But I'm not strong enough," I protested.

"Well, the next time you get tempted…" he began.

"That will be tonight," I interrupted, "because I'll be going home again."

"The next time you're tempted," he continued, "take a moment and go and stand out quietly somewhere on your own, and look up to God and let Him know how weak you are, but give Him permission to come into your mind at that moment."

I thought, "Wow! That sounds like something I could do." So I thanked him enthusiastically.

So that night, I came back. I turned left as usual. I walked past the dance hall. It was full. The lights were on. The band was playing. Dozens of people were in there—it was a big dance hall.

I paused at the gate of the dance hall, and a young woman who knew me rather well came out and saw me there.

"Oh, Bill, Bill," she called—and she came over and took hold of my arm and just led me into the hall.

Everything in me said, "No, no, no! I don't want to go in!" But my legs were saying, "Yes, yes, yes!" And, oh—I was so angry with myself! I got right to the door of the dance hall—right to the door—and I stopped dead in my tracks, because the Spirit brought Romans 6:16 back to my mind. "Quit struggling, quit resisting, quit fighting. Yield yourself to whom you will obey."

Yield. What's another word for yield? Surrender. "Quit struggling and surrender."

So I said to this girl, "Look, I'm not coming in at the moment. There's something I have to do."

"OK," she replied.

I turned around, and in front of this dance hall was a huge tree. I was 18 years of age, and this was the first time in my life I had ever done this. I went out and stood under that tree. I looked up into the sky and said to God, "You know, I'm about to go into the dance hall. I don't want to go into the dance hall, but I'm too weak. And the young preacher this morning told me that if I yielded my will to you, I wouldn't go into to the dance hall. I don't know how this is going to happen, but I'm giving you my will. You may have it."

Well, it's very hard to tell people what actually happens in a moment like that. But in one instant, you know what I knew? I knew I was not going into the dance hall. My weak human will was now fused with divinity. I didn't realize that. I had the mind of Christ in me, and Jesus was deciding not to go into the dance hall. And I turned around and began to walk away, and about a dozen of my friends came out looking for me. They stood in a circle around me. I'll never forget this.

"What are you doing out here on your own?"

Well, I was too embarrassed to tell them what I was doing. So I said, "Look—it's just that something's come up, and I can't come to the dance tonight."

They were very disappointed, but I walked off. I never went back to that dance hall again. I also learned one of the biggest lessons of my life. I learned that I could have struggled—I could have begged God to make me stronger. But in one moment of surrendering my will, God in me could do what I could not.

The only other lesson in that experience I had to learn was that I had to start turning right! Because I didn't need to be putting myself in the path of temptation. So I started turning right.

Well, a couple of years ago my older son, who's a pastor, was with me in Melbourne. He said, "Dad, take me out to where you used to live."

"Why?" I asked.

"Oh," he said, "I want to test something."

"OK," I agreed. So we took the train together out to where I used to live. We got off, and he said, "Dad, I know this will be tough for you, but I want you to empty your mind of all preconceived ideas."

"Oh, yeah, yeah," I said.

"I want you to walk through that gate," he said, "and without thinking, I just want you to automatically turn either to the left or the right."

"OK—no big deal," I said.

So I walked through the gate. I'm trying not to think about it. I'm just doing it very casually. Which way do you think I turned?

Of course, I turned right, because it had long since become a habit—hundreds of times I had turned right. In fact, I said to my son, "You know, it's interesting but I've actually forgotten how to go left. I'd have to go back and work out all the streets again, because for so long I turned right. And that is what is so simple for me. I can turn right and take you to the house where I used to live. It's no problem."

My eyes were truly opened regarding myself at that moment. Because I didn't have to think about it. I did by nature the thing that had been established in my life as a habit. And even though for years I had turned left, and that old pathway was still there, the establishment of the new pathway took over and kicked in.

And by the way, from my experience, this is of great importance. I think in the 12-Step programs they do a fearless, moral inventory. In other words, they teach people to identify habits that need to be replaced.

Don't live in generalities. It's a very healthy thing to identify habits in our lives that need to be replaced.

CHAPTER NINETEEN

All That You Need Is in Jesus

Do you understand that whatever you need to meet the problem of sin in your life is found in Jesus?

No matter what sin has done to you—whether it's placed you under the threat of death or condemnation, whether it's weakened you so you can't even make a right choice, whether it's led you to love things that are evil instead of things that are holy—it doesn't matter. Because the solution to all of those things is in Jesus Christ. And anyone who makes sure that they are in Christ every day of their lives will have His solution.

God will be "in you both to will and to work for His good pleasure." Philippians 2:13. Having begun a good work within you, He will bring it to completion. See Philippians 1:6.

Many Christians are failing, because instead of seeing their help in Christ, they try to *be* Christ. They want to overcome the devil personally. I know people whose whole ministry is to challenge the devil, to take him on, and to defeat him all the time. And I look at them with pity, because I know what's going to happen to them. They'll be sucked in by the devil. You can't take on the devil. He's already been taken on! He's been rendered powerless by the divine-human Man, Jesus Christ.

I know other people who are still falling back into the same habits after twenty years of praying, "God, make me strong enough to overcome." Only one human has ever been strong enough to overcome. The rest of us aren't strong enough! Only one human being has ever lived a life totally to the glory of God, by trusting in His Father.

And incredibly, because God is a God of grace, He has accepted that life of Jesus as my total life, and He makes that life available to me every day, by faith.

You want to be more loving today? Then you're not going to take a little seminar called, "How to Love Better." You're going to give the One who loved even His enemies (Matthew 5:43-48) the opportunity to come into your mind, and you're going to say to Him, "I give You permission today for Your mind to become one with mine, so that when I meet my enemies or those who are unlovely, You will love them through me."

You want to be more compassionate? Then you're going to let the One who couldn't even go to a funeral without being touched by the sorrow of a widow and wanting to raise her son (Luke 7:12-15)—you're going to let Him come into your mind. Even hanging on the cross, He was thinking of His own mother and handing her over to the tender care of John. John 19:25-27. So if you want compassion, you'll put Him on!

You want to be more generous? You have a problem with giving? Put on the One who didn't even have His own house—nowhere to lay His head. Matthew 8:20. Everything He had, He just gave. He accumulated nothing in terms of this world's goods. He didn't need it! He had everything from the Father. Yet He was totally satisfied. Put Him on. You'll become the most generous, splendid giver on earth, and you'll love to give. It will be a joy to give. You won't have to squeeze it out of yourself. At times you'll have to be held back from giving, lest you hurt yourself, because You'll have the One in you who loves to give! I'm serious.

You want to be at peace? Well, put on the One who, even though the storms were raging all around Him, would just go up into the mountaintop and communicate with His Father. Luke 6:11, 12. And His circumstances were not able to rob Him of peace. Jesus never hurried, you know—never rushed, never had to make decisions on the spur of the moment. Not at all! He carefully and quietly sought the will of His Father and with great peace of mind was able to face the most incredible temptations ever to confront a human being. We have not been called up into a mountain by the devil and asked to throw ourselves down. The devil hasn't done that to us. He has other ways of tricking us and deceiving us. But Jesus met him face to face for forty days.

You want to withstand temptation? Put on the One who, for forty days, simply said to the devil, "It is written. Man shall not live by bread alone. Thou shalt worship the Lord thy God." Jesus calmly answered Satan. He didn't get into debate with the devil. He simply quoted His Father's word and depended on it. Luke 4:1-13.

You want to be more evangelistic? Put on the One who couldn't walk into a little village without the whole village being turned upside down. Mark 2:1, 2. The sick were there, wanting to be healed (verse 3); the doubters were climbing trees to hear Him. Luke 19:1-4. He "did" evangelism wherever He went, because He had this great burden for souls.

You want to feel more hopeful? Put on the one who didn't even condemn Judas but kept offering him hope—and kept trying to reach his heart until the last. John 13:1-5. Put on the one who predicted that Peter would betray Him, then after Peter did, gave him the love and hope to get up and go on. Luke 22:31-34, 54-62; John 21:15-17.

Whatever you need at the human level, it's all in Christ! It's not in psychology. It's not in philosophy. It's not in self-improvement seminars. It's in Christ.

And if we were just willing to put on Christ every day—to submit ourselves to Him and give Him access to our minds—we would have everything Jesus has to offer. We'd be complete in Him. But what do we do? We struggle away. We get desperate. We try so hard to change our ways. We try. We fall. We beg God to help us. At times in desperation, we even blame Him for not having done more for us.

I remember years ago, when I actually said to God, "It doesn't work—this Christianity thing. It doesn't work. Look at me. I still have habits from when I became a believer."

And that's when He figuratively took a baseball bat and hit me over the head. He said, "I'm asking you to *put on* Christ, not to *be* Christ. There's only one human being who could take on the devil and overcome every temptation. And the Good News is—I have accepted you in Him! I've accepted His death as yours! I've accepted His life also as yours! I've accepted His resurrection as yours! You already have all these things. Tap into them! Avail yourself of all that Jesus has accomplished. It's all yours! Because I'm treating Jesus as if He were you—and you as if you were Jesus. I even allowed Him to become sin so that you wouldn't have to spend the rest of your life dealing with the sin problem. So you want victory? It's in Him."

If I stood up today and said, "I'm going to recruit a force to go to Vietnam," you'd all look at me and say, "You're crazy!" Because the war in Vietnam is over. It's been fought already.

Or maybe I'd say that I'm going to take you back to the battlefields of World War II. "Let's go fight the Nazis!" And you'd all say, "What? That war's been fought and won already!"

But what are Christians doing today? They're gathering their forces to fight a fight that's already been won!

Our fight is the fight of faith! It's not the fight against sin. That's been fought and won in human strength by a Man who depended fully on His Father. Our fight is not against the devil. He's already been overcome and declared powerless. You'd never guess it, though, the way Christians are relating to him. You'd think he had all the power!

Some parents came to me and said, "Ohhh! The devil's got our son."

"Well," I said, "what are you going to do about it?"

Then I added, "Do you realize that your son's been taken by a powerless foe who somehow has convinced you that he's got power? What are you going to do about it? Are you going to take it sitting down? Are you going to say, 'What can we do?' Or by faith are you going to move forward and say, 'Hey! You think you've snared my son, but I've got news for you. You have no authority here. I'm claiming him back in the name of Jesus Christ. And I'm going to be claiming him back until he's delivered right back here to me. You have no power and authority over him."

I don't see many people acting by faith today. They're acting as if the enemy now has all the cards, and he's playing them. He's the master of deception. He has no authority. We act as if he has us out-powered and out-maneuvered. And the Bible says he's been rendered powerless. Think about that—powerless. Hebrews 2:14.

So if you're seeking and struggling for victory with help from God, you'll be digging the same hole twenty years from now. But if you're seeking victory through putting on Christ, you'll have it now!

CHAPTER TWENTY

Victory Through Surrender

Please notice in the following passage who is doing the speaking:

"Then he showed me Joshua the high priest standing before the angel of the **Lord,** and Satan standing at his right hand to accuse him. The **Lord** said to Satan, 'The **Lord** rebuke you, Satan! Indeed, the **Lord** who has chosen Jerusalem rebuke you! Is this not a brand plucked from the fire?'" Zechariah 3:1, 2, emphasis supplied.

Did you see it? "The *Lord* rebuke you, Satan." The power and authority to rebuke Satan is in Christ. It's in Christ. So it would appear that I'm not rebuking Satan, but the Lord is rebuking Satan. So I think these are words that we could well use: "The Lord rebuke you, Satan."

And every time I read this, I remind myself that power and authority against Satan is not in or from me. It's in Christ—and it's Christ who actually rebukes the devil. So it's OK in the name of Jesus to say, "The Lord rebuke you, Satan." But it's not OK to say that *I'm* rebuking you—even in the authority of God. I think that's a dangerous course of action.

Unfortunately, there are a lot of people who move into that approach today. And I've seen what's happened to them. But it's a totally different matter to realize that it's the Lord who has rebuked Satan, and to claim that by faith.

As I said to the parents in the previous chapter who felt the devil had their son: "The enemy is only deceiving you into thinking that this is a struggle between you and him, because he knows that the real struggle was between Christ and him—and he lost that struggle. He doesn't ever want you to find that out, so that you will continue to feel that somehow now, you have to meet him and take him on. And you don't. You simply need to move into belief."

Even when it comes to victory over sins in our lives, it's not our struggle! Our struggle, again, is to move into faith and to believe that in human flesh—and I mean a flesh that God has accepted as mine!—Jesus overcame all temptation. In principle, He's already met the temptations I am meeting, and my victory over them is to see that in human flesh, He has already accomplished this, and to put Him on.

And when you put on Christ and invite Him into your life, what kind of person are you putting on? You're putting on Someone who is not drawn to evil. You're putting on Someone who's already victorious.

Look at the powerful words in 1 John that reinforce this. 1 John 5:4: "For whatever is born of God overcomes the world; and this is the victory that has overcome the world—our faith."

"For whatever is…struggling 'til the very end." Is that how your version reads? No. "Whatever is born of God…"

I hope you're seeing that victory is a faith experience, not a struggling experience. Instead of struggling, the victorious actually surrender.

I'm challenging in these pages the idea that—if only I can somehow get enough power and help from God to go with my own efforts—I can overcome the devil. I'm firmly challenging this idea. Actually, I'm more than challenging it—I'm rejecting it! Because in my spiritual life, I'm giving up even the right to fight the devil. I'm giving that up to Christ. I'm acknowledging that I can't fight the devil, because I am powerless—helpless! I am surrendering to Jesus Christ the right to take on the devil and temptation and sin. That's what I'm doing the moment I move into faith. I'm actually saying to God, "I can't do this. Thank You for providing Jesus."

From Fighting to Faith

In most battles, victory comes through fighting to win. But not in our spiritual lives. Here, victory comes not through fighting, but through surrendering! And what do we surrender? The very thought that we might have any right to take on the devil. The very hope that we might have any chance of success against him. Instead, we recognize that God has provided for us One who's not only taken on the devil, but has successfully overcome him in human flesh. And when we put on Jesus, His success, His victory, becomes ours.

So when we're facing temptation, sin, and the devil, instead of fighting and struggling—which we've all done for years, almost to the point of total discouragement at times—we move instead into faith, and we look at what the Son of Man has accomplished already in human flesh.

The toughest thing for most of us to accept is that in the resolution of the sin problem—whether it's dealing with condemnation and death, or whether it's dealing with sin as a power in our lives—God has placed the responsibility for resolving that upon Jesus, not upon us.

So when I'm tempted, I move into faith. Another way of saying that is that I surrender my right to take on sin and the devil and allow Jesus to do what He was asked to do by the Father. And if we're reading 1 John correctly here, whoever is born of God overcomes the world. So when you're born of God, you are putting on Jesus Christ. Through the Spirit, you are receiving the mind of Christ. Now, it is Christ in you who overcomes the world—not you in your natural human flesh.

This is a faith experience.

God in you! If you're born of God, you have God in you! The gospel is not just the story of God—it's the *power* of God unto salvation. God will indwell any human being who enters into belief regarding His love gift of Jesus Christ.

I've decided that few people, apparently, really believe in Jesus as the Son of God. I can't even get people to testify about justification today. They won't say it. They won't praise God for it. Yet this is what it means to believe that Jesus is the Son of God—that God has accepted His perfect life and death as mine! I am no longer considered guilty, condemned, and under death. I have the title deed to heaven. I've entered into the family of God. I'm His child!

Consider just a couple of the Bible promises that support this truth:

"But as many as received Him, to them He gave the right to become children of God, even to those who believe in His name." John 1:12.

"Whoever confesses that Jesus is the Son of God, God abides in him, and he in God." 1 John 4:15.

What does it take for God to abide in us—to dwell in us? Our confession that Jesus is the Son of God. That's why I keep emphasizing that the most important habit in your life is to come to the cross every morning, look at the cross, and say, "Thank You, God, for sending Your own Son in human flesh and allowing Him to take upon Himself the responsibility for sin. I do believe it with all my heart."

And the moment you say it, God is in you. You walk out of your house with the presence of the living God in you. And I've decided there aren't many people doing this. Because people walk up and say, "Oh, I've got this problem with my bad temper…" "Oh, I'm getting angry all the time…" "Oh, I've got this habit…"

I met a pastor a while back. He said, "I've just got this pornography habit, and it's killing me."

I said to him, "Let me find my tissue here so I can weep for you."

"I'm serious," he said.

"So am I," I replied. "I'm not weeping for you because you've got a problem. I'm weeping for you because you don't understand faith! You're not confessing every day of your life that Jesus is the Son of God! Because if you were, you'd have the mind of Christ, and hallelujah, you might just be able to look at a gorgeous woman without lusting. You might actually be able to look and say, 'Thank You, God, for this beautiful creation. I don't see her as an object of lust. I see her as a beautiful creation coming forth from Your hand.'"

I want to tell you, the first time this happened to me, I said, "Thank You, God!"

"Well," God told me, "just keep My mind in you, and you can have this quality of thought every day of your life."

But this pastor was telling me, "Oh, please help me! I'm just looking at pornography every day. It's killing me."

"Well, it would kill me, too, to feed my mind on that!" I said to him. "Have you ever wondered, if you had the mind of Christ, you might just have the strength to put a filter on your computer—that if you just confessed Jesus Christ, then, with the mind of Christ in you, you could go home and order a filter?"

And this pastor looked at me in amazement.

"That's what it would take," I told him. "I'm not going to do it for you. You are out of faith. You're out of faith when you come to me with a statement like that."

Another man stood up in one of my seminars and said, "I'm an addict to television. For twenty years I've just come home at five o'clock in the afternoon, put my feet up, and then gone to bed at twelve o'clock at night. For that whole time, I haven't moved. I have no marriage to speak of. My wife and I are like two strangers living in a house together. I don't even know why she stays."

Luckily, his wife wasn't present.

"I'm just so weak and miserable," he added. "Do you have any wisdom for me?"

"Of course, I do—of course. But," I said, "it would take the mind of Christ. You're out of faith! You're wrestling and struggling with something that Jesus Christ would not have a problem with, because He wasn't drawn to violence and sex and all those things that fill up the television stations. He had a healthy balance in His life. Oh, He enjoyed the company of women. Of course, He did. Why do you think He spent so much time at Mary and Martha's house? I think He found there a love that He hadn't found anywhere else. But He wasn't into the perverted view of these things, and if you put His mind on …"

"Well," he interrupted, "what would happen if I put on the mind of Christ?"

"With the mind of Christ," I answered, "you'd look at the television set and you'd say, 'OK, this is controlling my life.' So probably you'd take out a pair of scissors, and you'd probably cut the cord."

I could see he was listening carefully.

"Quit struggling," I continued. "Start surrendering. Start surrendering and put on the mind of Christ. Enter into belief that Jesus has overcome the world, the flesh, and the devil! In human flesh He's done this! Confess it! And where will Christ be from that moment? He'll be in your mind. That's the part of you with which the Holy Spirit makes contact. And with Christ in your mind, you're going to make the right decision regarding television."

So he went home that week, and he did it. He came back the next week, and he was jumping up and down like I've never seen. You should have heard his testimony. He said, "For twenty years I've been a slave. But I put on the mind of Christ, and I knew exactly what I needed to do. I took out a pair of scissors, and I cut off the plug—and there it stays, because I acknowledged that I could not handle that set. It was handling me."

Then his eyes lighted up, and he said, "I feel free—and my wife and I are starting to dialog together. I've just revived in the Spirit. I'm no longer a slave to sin, because I've put on the mind of Christ."

With Christ's mind, you see things differently. Yet you realize how easy it is to cross over the line and go back to doing things the old carnal way instead of God's way. I can't go one day of my life without seeking the mind of Christ, because the world is not safe. I may be intolerant of people, yet with Christ in me I find the most incredible grace coming through to be tolerant of people and understanding and loving. That is His way.

And what He wants all of us to do is to put Him on with such regularity that these things will become habitual and natural in our lives.

Just recently, I realized that something I used to find attractive no longer was. I couldn't actually put my finger on just when it had happened, because it had apparently just taken place over a period of time

So I looked up and said, "Thank you, God!"

And He said, "Well, you didn't notice it happening, because you've been focused on putting on Christ."

Gradually, Christ's desires become ours by nature. That's when it gets exciting. And what do we call that whole process? Sanctification.

How Sanctification Works

And in that process, notice that if you find yourself repeating the same habits over and over again, you probably have fallen out of faith. And you need to move back into confessing that Jesus is the Son of God, and the moment you do that, you move out of the old habits into strengthening new ones.

When I first started to understand this, I had to make this confession a number of times a day. And every time I felt the temptation, or the old things coming back, I found myself increasingly wanting to move into confession that I do believe that Jesus is the Son of the living God, and in human flesh overcame sin, temptation, the flesh, the world!

The moment we confess that Jesus is the Son, and we praise

God for His love gift, God abides in us. The bottom line is—it's God in you who resists sin, not you plus some help from God. God is the only being who is not drawn to unholiness. By nature, we are drawn to the unholy. God is not. So if you find yourself not being drawn to the unholy, you'll know that God is in you. And you'll say, "Yes! Praise the Lord!"

The biggest struggle of our lives is whether to surrender and give God permission to be in us so we will not be drawn to the unholy—or whether to fight against being drawn to the unholy and beg God to make us strong enough to do it. This last way is the path of failure, and it's led many Christians to be focused on their sins and to be unable to change themselves.

Armor for Protection, Not Battle

You know, the armor of God (see Ephesians 6:10-17) is not put on so you can do battle with Satan. The armor of God is put on to protect you from the darts of the enemy. Some people think you put on the armor to do battle with Satan. You don't. It's for your protection that you put it on.

The battle has been won. But it goes on in us, because our struggle is whether to believe it or not—or whether to continue on in our own self-defeating ways. These two approaches are light and darkness. One results in victory—the other results in defeat.

Victory in the Christian life comes through surrendering our right to fight sin and the devil, moving into belief that this fight was put on Jesus Christ, and confessing that we believe this. And the moment we do, the Spirit of the living God brings Christ into our minds. We now have the mind of Christ. And the mind of Christ is not drawn to sin and evil. It is drawn to the things that are holy and pure.

Too many people work at resisting sin and the devil, trying hard not to give in to temptation, begging God to give them strength so that they will not yield. Then, when they fall back, they get really discouraged and start to question whether, in fact, God means what He says or not.

And they always end up blaming God or deciding they are just too weak and are not going to make it. When people reach that point, you know what they say to themselves? "Well, it doesn't matter whether I even try." And they start allowing everything to come back into their lives again. They even give up the struggle. I've known many that have been there, because they can't be strong enough to resist temptation and the devil, even with help from God.

So finally, one day by the grace of God, in their utmost despair, they fall at the foot of the cross. Then they realize, "God has asked Jesus to do this—not me. It's my privilege to take hold of Him by faith and to have Him in me. It's God in me who resists evil—not me."

If I'm not successfully resisting evil, chances are God's not in me, because I'm doing it in my own strength instead of by faith—and through allowing Him to come into me.

In the four chapters of Romans 5 through 8, Paul comes to grips with the characteristics of people who claim to be believers, yet are still carnal. But Paul makes a distinction between professed believers who are still carnal—and professed believers who are spiritual but still appear to have some very interesting characteristics.

And there's a lot of confusion out there as to what really happens when a person becomes spiritual. Some people think, for example, that they'll never feel tempted again. Others think they will never ever feel an inclination to sin again. Some think they'll never be drawn by anything unattractive again. And they're shocked if they find this happening to themselves, and they immediately start thinking, "I must be carnal."

It's interesting to me that Paul called the believers in Corinth "saints." Yet were they fully mature in Christ? Oh, no.

So apparently, you can be in Christ, and be in process of becoming mature, without being called carnal. You could even have a day where things come out that shock you when you hear them, and still not be back in the carnal realm. Because remember—you are under grace. And when you're under grace, there is freedom now to grow up into Christ and address every aspect of your life, without feeling condemned!

If you're under grace, you are free to address every aspect of your life and character, and you're free to grow up and mature in every way, without feeling condemned as you go through this.

Now is that Good News—or what?

CHAPTER TWENTY-ONE

Carnal—or Spiritual?

I had a young man approach me recently who was seriously in shock because he was experiencing some sexual feelings going on in his body. And he came to me and said, "You know, I must be carnal."

"Well," I told him, "I've got good news for you. You happen to be a normal male. That's the good news. You're a normal member of the male species. And God made your body this way. It's biochemistry, and you are designed to respond a certain way. It is not carnality.

It's what you do with these desires that reflects whether you are carnal or spiritual. And the spiritual man, just because he feels promptings within his body, doesn't necessarily run out to satisfy his every need. A spiritual man learns to keep his body under subjection. He's not dominated and controlled by his physical urges. He actually praises God. And you ought to be praising God that you're normal!"

What matters is the mind. And why does the Holy Spirit make contact with the mind? The Bible says, "Let this mind be in you, which was also in Christ Jesus." Philippians 2:5, KJV. Also: "Be transformed by the renewing of your mind." Romans 12:2. It's the mind that is renewed! When you move into belief, and you confess that Jesus is the Christ, the Son of the Living God, the Holy Spirit comes again for that day and renews your mind.

God gives you new thoughts. You might have hated someone your whole life, and God will give you a new feeling toward that person. Compassion will be there. Suddenly you are confronted with a new standard in your life—the life of Christ.

University of the Mind

Our mind is like a university. It has all these faculties. There's the area of reason—there's the area of appetite. Some people think that if they're born again, they should never have a temptation of appetite again. There's an area that has all the senses in it—seeing, hearing, smelling, touching. And the sexual area of our lives is controlled by a faculty of the mind. There's the area of the will. And of course, the area of emotions.

So what are we receiving new when Christ's mind is in us? New thoughts, feelings, and motives. That's what God is putting into your mind when He puts the mind of Christ in you. You don't have to try finding good motives. God will give you the right motives if you put on the mind of Christ. You don't have to work at changing your feelings. God will give you new feelings. And He'll give you new thoughts. He'll take you to a much higher level than you've been to before.

Think of the area concerning sexual motivation. To the young man I mentioned as this chapter began, I said, "As you seek the mind of Christ, the area that controls sexual activity in your brain is going to see that this is a gift from God that is to be used in such a way, when you enter into marriage, that it will bring about a unity resembling the relationship between the members of the trinity. This will be a thought that will have never entered into your mind until now. It will be the mind of Christ in you."

This particular faculty will now be aroused to action in totally different ways. It doesn't matter what Hollywood says, or what all the glossy magazines say, God will be putting His ideal within you now.

What about appetite? Suddenly, those who are making food their God, or those who are using it as a means of salvation, will find that the faculty that controls appetite is going to show them a totally new perspective on appetite. They're going to see the importance of health, but it's not going to become their means of their salvation. It's now going to be in the context of their total development, to the glory of God. Those who've been overindulging appetite will now be shown that self-control is possible in the area of appetite. They will no longer be dominated by the thought, "I can't do anything about it"—because that faculty will now be aroused to action in new lines.

So you are not given new faculties. The faculty of appetite doesn't just suddenly change so that all you want now is perfect use of your appetite. It doesn't happen. But the faculties are sanctified.

In a sudden moment, it came clear to me: "Oh, I see—sanctification takes place in the mind. Sanctification takes place in the mind!"

If a faculty of my mind is aroused to action in new lines and my will is strengthened by Christ being in me, what if I then choose to act upon that new line of action? And what if I choose to act upon it regularly in my life? What will obviously happen in the faculty? It will be ennobled and sanctified, so that ultimately it is my natural inclination. It will become habitual in my life. This is the miracle of God's grace.

Now notice this beautiful statement from *The Desire of Ages*, page 668:

> "All true obedience comes from the heart. It was heart work with Christ. And if we consent, He will so identify Himself with our thoughts and aims, so blend our hearts and minds into conformity to His will, that when obeying Him we shall be but carrying out our own impulses."

Think about that. If you permit, Christ will so identify with your mind that in just doing what comes naturally now, you'll be doing His will! That's a beautiful thought, isn't it?

Even in thinking your own thoughts, you're thinking Christ's. This is the process of sanctification. And I want to tell you, it comes about by habitually responding to what the Holy Spirit has placed in your mind.

Now I have a question for you. What happens in the lives of true, spiritual believers after conversion? What kind of feelings do they have? What kind of temptations do they have? What is their attitude? On the other hand, what I want to know is—what are the experiences, the characteristics of a person who claims to be a believer in Christ, but is still carnal?

One or the Other—but Not Both

The Good News is, you cannot be both carnal and spiritual. You can only be one or the other. As we take a closer look here, we're going to find that a truly spiritual person has some rather interesting characteristics. And some of us may be tempted to confuse those with being carnal.

It's like that young man that came to me. He wasn't carnal at all. He was quite spiritual, but he thought he was carnal.

Romans 5 through 8 are the only chapters in scripture, really, that bring this out in any depth. And particularly, the passage between Romans 7:21 and Romans 8:8 helps everything else Paul is saying to fall into place. This is not an easy passage—especially chapter 7. But if you hear what Paul is saying, suddenly reality will strike you. It took me twenty-five years to understand this passage, but it doesn't need to take that long!

Focus now on Romans 7:25: "Thanks be to God through Jesus Christ our Lord! So then, on the one hand I myself with my mind am serving the law of God, but on the other, with my flesh the law of sin."

Please note that this verse is not suggesting that Paul is doing

Carnal—or Spiritual? • 155

both of these things simultaneously. You need to read what precedes verse 25 and what immediately follows it. If you're thinking that he's saying he's doing these two things at the same time, you haven't heard what he has said before it or what comes immediately after it. And this is where most people run afoul in this passage. They think, "Well, how can you be serving both at the same time?"

You cannot! And you must allow verse 25 to be interpreted by what comes before it and what comes immediately after it. If you carefully study the context, you'll know exactly what Paul is trying to tell you. The key is in those verses.

Something very interesting comes out of Romans 7—the most misunderstood chapter Paul ever wrote. It's been the source of contention between theologians for 2,000 years and continues to be so. Even when I was at seminary, the professors were divided. One professor told us all that in Romans 7:25, Paul was in an unconverted state. The next professor told us that this was Paul in a converted state. And we were left hanging. They would not commit themselves.

I want you to notice now some rather interesting facts. I'm going back to verses 16 to 18 in chapter 7: "But if I do the very thing I do not want to do, I agree with the Law, confessing that the Law is good. So now, no longer am I the one doing it, but sin which dwells in me. For I know that nothing good dwells in me, that is, in my flesh."

I hope you saw these words: "I know that nothing good dwells in me." The words of what kind of man? You'll never hear a carnal man acknowledge that. Of course, you won't. These are the words of a spiritual man.

One of the "big ideas" we spent time discussing earlier in this book concerned our basic condition: helpless, powerless, sinful. And I want to tell you, the recognition and affirmation of that condition is the first step in the life of a person who turns to Jesus Christ. Such people become convicted of their true condition.

"I know that nothing good dwells in me."

That's a point of enlightenment that the vast majority of the human race never reach. No good thing. So very important.

And the first thing we notice in our passage of Romans 7 is that Paul is making a profound acknowledgement about himself. He's well aware of what sin has done to his human nature.

"For I know that nothing good dwells in me, that is, in my flesh; for the willing is present in me, but the doing of the good is not." Verse 18.

If someone says the desire is present within them, what is he acknowledging? The carnal mind "is not subject to the law of God," nor can be. Romans 8:7, KJV. But here we have a man who is wishing to do right. On one hand, he's acknowledging the truth of his own sinfulness, and on the other hand, acknowledging that he really wants to do right. But he's struggling! He is struggling to do right. Sound familiar to most of you?

Oh, yes, he's struggling to do it. There's no way that we're talking about a man here who's not spiritual. He's acknowledging his true condition and the fact that, even as a believer—a spiritual person and a true believer—there is a struggle going on within himself.

So what's new? I never had a struggle until I became a believer. I used to just enjoy sin. I didn't even know it was sin! I just thought it was life. But then I became a believer, and oh, how things changed!

There is a struggle within spiritual believers. We have to acknowledge it. And it's important for us to identify the two sides of this struggle that go on within the life of a true believer.

It's time now to zero in closely on the context in Romans and allow Paul himself to give us the correct understanding of chapter 7, verse 25, where he describes the struggle he is having with the "law of God" and the "law of sin."

Let's first look, before verse 25, at chapter 7, verses 21-23: "I find then the principle that evil is present in me, the one who wants to do good. For I joyfully concur with the law of God in the inner man, but I see a different law in the members of my body, waging war against the law of my mind and making me a prisoner of the law of sin which is in my members."

So here I have, on one hand, the law of my mind—or the law of God in the inner man. And on the other hand, the law of sin in the members of my body.

And now here's chapter 8, verse 2, coming after chapter 7:25: "For the law of the Spirit of life in Christ Jesus has set you free from the law of sin and of death."

So now we can see that Paul is equating the "law of sin" in chapter 7, verse 25, with "the law in the members of my body" and the "law of sin and death."

And Paul's description of the "law of God"? It's "the law of God in the inner man," "the law of my mind," and "the law of the Spirit of life in Christ Jesus."

Once you understand what Paul is really saying here about these two conflicting laws, it will revolutionize your life—because there is a struggle! Yes, there is! In fact, this kind of struggle—dare I suggest it—is only present in the experience of a truly spiritual person, a converted individual, someone who's born again into the kingdom of God. This is the only category of person on this earth that experiences this kind of struggle. This is also the reason that same category of person is in the gravest danger of becoming unstable. Because if you don't resolve this struggle, you remain like a house divided for the rest of your life, and you can de-stabilize yourself.

It took me years to realize that people become unstable when they're convicted one way—but they act differently. That sets up confusion in the human mind.

Does Paul resolve this struggle here? Yes, he does! There is a very real struggle going on in the experience of the true spiritual believer. And it is interesting what the struggle is. It's a struggle between the law of my mind and the law in the members of my body. It's a struggle between the law of the spirit of life in Christ

Jesus (in my mind)—and the law of sin and death (in the members of my body).

Now, I'm sure Paul had a limited understanding of physiology, but he's endeavoring to teach us something very powerful here—that the struggle in the life of the believer is a struggle between the mind, which is now the mind of Christ, and the members of our bodies, which could bring us under the law of sin and death.

In our next and final chapter, we will explore more fully Paul's teaching about the carnal man—and the spiritual man.

CHAPTER TWENTY-TWO

The Old—and the New

Even someone who is spiritual will find that the flesh continues to make war against the spirit. You should not expect to reach a point where you never feel some inclination toward sin within you.

Reality for the spiritual man is that a struggle is in place, because, on one hand, he's now born of the Spirit, and in his mind he has the law of the Spirit of Christ. But on the other hand, he feels in the members of his body an impulse to sin.

So what, specifically, is it from which he looks for deliverance? The wishing to do good is present with him, but the doing of the good—well, he may not be having a lot of success in that area. He has the desire to do God's will within him, but the doing of it is not present.

See how Paul puts it here in Romans 7:24: "Wretched man that I am! Who will set me free from the body of this death?"

In other words, I can have the mind of Christ, yet I'm feeling the promptings to sin in my body. Who is going to set me free from the fact that I find myself unable to do what the Spirit is prompting me to do?

Time now to revisit Romans 8:2: "For the law of the Spirit of life in Christ Jesus has set you free from the law of sin and of death." Now, it's interesting that Paul precedes these words by one other thought. Because in verse 1 he's also told us something else: "Therefore there is now no condemnation for those who are in Christ Jesus."

Condemnation, as we learned earlier in this book, is related to the death of Jesus Christ. It was our condemnation that fell on Him and caused His death. This is belief in the death of Jesus. If you're free from condemnation you've moved into belief in the death of Jesus.

So we have the life and death of Jesus Christ now becoming the means by which our struggle is resolved! Because as long as you live in the body, you will feel the ever-presence of sin within you. But the resolution of the struggle is to move into belief regarding the death of Jesus, which immediately opens the door for you to receive His life in you!

The struggle is resolved by faith—faith in the death and resurrection of Jesus. If you move into faith in the death of Jesus, even though you feel the promptings to sin within you, you will know that you are not condemned. Then, if you put on the life of Christ—this is *His* life, now—what will actually happen?

Walking After the Spirit

You will now begin to walk after the Spirit. And if you walk after the Spirit habitually, what will happen? What will the final result be? You'll have the mind of Christ. The faculties of your mind will be sanctified.

Notice now Romans 8:13: "For if you are living according to the flesh, you must die; but if by the Spirit you are putting to death the deeds of the body, you will live."

And notice too the tense of the verb in this verse. It doesn't say that you have already put (past tense) all the deeds of the body to death. No, it's in the continuous or present tense: "you are putting to death the deeds of the body."

Let me also bring in here Galatians 5:16-18: "But I say, walk by the Spirit, and you will not carry out the desire of the flesh. For the flesh sets its desire against the Spirit, and the Spirit against the flesh; for these are in opposition to one another, so that you may not do the things that you please. But if you are led by the Spirit, you are not under the Law." What a beautiful statement! It's a summary, really, of what we just read in Romans.

Most people of my acquaintance are failing in their spiritual walk, because they don't develop consistent habits of walking in the Spirit. The only way you can resist walking in the flesh is to have daily the mind of Christ—to have your mind renewed daily. It's a daily—actually, a moment-by-moment—renewal. You may have to renew your mind constantly through the day—having the mind of Christ. Because you *will* feel things within you. But this is not a sign that you're carnal. Because if you're even sensitive to those things within you, that's an evidence that you're spiritual!

But it's vital that you choose to develop new and regular habits. Remember the man I mentioned earlier in this book who cut his television cord? I said to him, "Why don't you develop the habit now of reading uplifting literature?"

He has indeed begun the habit of reading. I heard his testimony again recently, and I was just praising God.

"I've developed a love for incredible literature," he said. "I'd forgotten how to read. I used to sit down in front of the tube. Now I'm reading, and I'm rejoicing."

So this man did not just eliminate a bad habit, he began filling the vacuum with something positive.

Consider his old pathway—his old habit. He walked into his house. Immediately, the habit kicked in. He'd sit down on the sofa. His wife would bring him his dinner on a tray. And he'd put his feet up and lie there for five or six hours.

But now when he walks into his home, the cord is cut. Now, he's actually doing things with his wife around the house. And when he is free, he picks up a good book and sits down to read it.

When he gets home these days, the old pathway no longer kicks in. Why not? Because he has now developed over a period of time a different pathway.

When he comes home, this new pathway kicks in, and now he's reading things that glorify God. He told me, "I don't even want to watch television."

"Hallelujah!" I replied.

The new pathway has kicked in and taken over from the old. His faculty—especially the faculty of how he used his eyes and his ears—has been sanctified. He now wants to read and look at and hear things that are uplifting and holy and ennobling.

So Simple We Sometimes Miss It

That's how simple it is. It's so simple that most of us miss it. We get discouraged because we still feel the promptings to sin within us. And we say, "I must be still carnal. I'm just not making it."

And we also fail in a second way. We don't consistently set about establishing new habits in our lives that will glorify God. We allow the old pathways to be kicked into place. And they're triggered by things out there.

Perhaps you're looking at your own life and saying, "Oh, now I can see why I've had these moments of discouragement. I can see why I may even have felt that I'm never going to be victorious. Or why I've never used the word *victory* in my entire life. Or why I've never really even realized the possibility of what I could be in Christ.

But now I'm actually understanding the apostle Paul here, who's describing the reality—the real experience—of spiritual people who still feel the pull of sin in their flesh and yet, by faith, take hold of the death of Jesus. And they're free now from condemnation and free to put on the mind of Christ every day.

And once the mind of Christ is in us, we walk now according to the Spirit, and we walk consistently—to the point where we develop habits in our lives that become our natural way of functioning. And the faculties of our mind are becoming sanctified.

If you're putting on the mind of Christ daily, you'll have the same care and concern for others. But it will be Christ in you concerning Himself in ministry for others, and this gives Him freedom to take your personal encounters to any depth He knows is necessary. You won't have to worry, "Should I go further here, or should I go further there?" You can simply focus on putting on the mind of Christ, and let Him guide the ministry and develop it. You'll know exactly how far to go and to what degree you can intercede and care and pray for other people. It'll be perfectly clear, once the mind of Christ is present in you every day.

Until I started putting on the mind of Christ I never had clarity in my mind on most of these ministry issues. But once I started putting on the mind of Christ and giving Him access every day, I could see immediately what to do and how far to go and when to intercede and when to pray and when not to—even at times not praying when people were begging me to pray. But God said to me, "Now, don't get too confident about this. Remember—it's not you. It's Me *in* you. That's My understanding coming through."

As this book ends, I'd like to end it with a prayer:

"Father in heaven, thank You so much for being with us as we've journeyed together through these pages. Thank You for the incredible pictures of You that have come out—and for the joy that we can have in Jesus Christ.

"We claim by faith just now, the covering of His shed blood, knowing that by looking to the cross, we can believe ourselves to be free from condemnation. Thank You too, Father, for the awareness we've developed, that within the life of a spiritual person is the continual struggle as the flesh tries to manifest itself against the Spirit. But we know that with Paul, we can claim that same victory: 'Thanks be to God,' he said. 'There is therefore now no condemnation for those who are in Christ Jesus, because the Spirit of the law of the life of Christ has set us free from the law of sin and death.'

"And we close these pages today, knowing that now, we have the mind of Christ. Give us the grace, Father, to establish habits in our lives that will give You the glory, so that our faculties may be sanctified. And when You come, we will look like You, because we'll have Your mind.

"Thank You, Father, in anticipation of all these blessings. In Jesus' precious name, Amen."

Appendix

Article entitled "Genuine Conversion," by Ellen G. White, published in the *Review and Herald*, July 7, 1904:

In order to be saved, we must know by experience the meaning of true conversion. It is a fearful mistake for men and women to go on day by day, professing to be Christians, yet having no right to the name. In God's sight, profession is nothing, position is nothing. He asks, Is the life in harmony with my precepts?

There are many who suppose that they are converted, but who are not able to bear the test of character presented in the Word of God. Sad will it be, in the day when every man is rewarded according to his works, for those who can not bear this test.

Conversion is a change of heart, a turning from unrighteousness to righteousness. Relying upon the merits of Christ, exercising true faith in him, the repentant sinner receives pardon for sin. As he ceases to do evil, and learns to do well, he grows in grace and in the knowledge of God. He sees that in order to follow Jesus

---

For additional information about Ellen G. White and her writings, see the website at: www.whiteestate.org.

he must separate from the world, and, after counting the cost, he looks upon all as loss if he may but win Christ. He enlists in his army, and bravely and cheerfully engages in the warfare, fighting against natural inclinations and selfish desires, and bringing the will into subjection to the will of Christ. Daily he seeks the Lord for grace, and he is strengthened and helped. Self once reigned in his heart, and worldly pleasure was his delight. Now self is dethroned, and God reigns supreme. His life reveals the fruit of righteousness. The sins he once loved he now hates. Firmly and resolutely he follows in the path of holiness. This is genuine conversion.

In the lives of many of those whose names are on the church books there has been no genuine change. The truth has been kept in the outer court. There has been no genuine conversion, no positive work of grace done in the heart. Their desire to do God's will is based upon their own inclination, not upon the deep conviction of the Holy Spirit. Their conduct is not brought into harmony with the law of God. They profess to accept Christ as their Saviour, but they do not believe that he will give them power to overcome their sins. They have not a personal acquaintance with a living Saviour, and their characters reveal many blemishes.

Many a one who looks at himself in the divine mirror, and is convinced that his life is not what it ought to be, fails to make the needed change. He goes his way, and forgets his defects. He may profess to be a follower of Christ, but what does this avail if his character has undergone no change, if the Holy Spirit has not wrought upon his heart? The work done has been superficial. Self is retained in his life. He is not a partaker of the divine nature. He may talk of God and pray to God, but his life reveals that he is working against God.

Let us not forget that in his conversion and sanctification, man must cooperate with God. "Work out your own salvation with fear and trembling," the Word declares; "for it is God which worketh in you both to will and to do of his good pleasure." Man can not transform himself by the exercise of his will. He possesses no power by which this change may be effected. The renewing energy must come from God. The change can be made only by the Holy Spirit. He who would be saved, high or low, rich or poor, must submit to the working of this power.

As the leaven, when mingled with the meal, works from within outward, so it is by the renewing of the heart that the grace of God works to transform the life. No mere external change is sufficient to bring us into harmony with God. There are many who try to reform by correcting this bad habit or that bad habit, and they hope in this way to become Christians, but they are beginning in the wrong place. Our first work is with the heart.

The great truth of the conversion of the heart by the Holy Spirit is presented in Christ's words to Nicodemus: "Verily, verily, I say unto thee, Except a man be born from above, he can not see the kingdom of God. . . . That which is born of the flesh is flesh; and that which is born of the Spirit is spirit. Marvel not that I said unto thee, Ye must be born again. The wind bloweth where it listeth, and thou hearest the sound thereof, but canst not tell whence it cometh, and whither it goeth: so is every one that is born of the Spirit."

The leaven of truth works secretly, silently, steadily, to transform the soul. The natural inclinations are softened and subdued. New thoughts, new feelings, new motives, are implanted. A new standard of character is set up,--the life of Christ. The mind is changed; the faculties are aroused to action in new lines. Man is not endowed with new faculties, but the faculties he has are sanctified. The conscience is awakened.

The Scriptures are the great agency in this transformation of character. Christ prayed, "Sanctify them through thy truth: thy word is truth." If studied and obeyed, the word of God works in the heart, subduing every unholy attribute. The Holy Spirit comes to convict of sin, and the faith that springs up in the heart works by love to Christ, conforming us, body, soul, and spirit, to his will.

A man sees his danger. He sees that he needs a change of character, a change of heart. He is stirred; his fears are aroused. The

Spirit of God is working in him, and with fear and trembling he works for himself, seeking to find out his defects of character, and to see what he can do to bring about the needed change in his life. His heart is humbled. By confession and repentance he shows the sincerity of his desire to reform. He confesses his sins to God, and if he has injured any one, he confesses the wrong to the one he has injured. While God is working, the sinner, under the influence of the Holy Spirit, works out that which God is working in mind and heart. He acts in harmony with the Spirit's working, and his conversion is genuine.

The nobility and dignity of the man increase as he takes his position against the wily foe, who for so many years has kept him in slavery. He feels a holy indignation arising within him as he thinks that for so long he has been Satan's bond-slave, allowing the enemy to lead him to refuse to acknowledge his best friend.

Let the sinner co-operate with his Redeemer to secure his liberty. Let him be assured that unseen heavenly agencies are working in his behalf. Dear souls in doubt and discouragement, pray for the courage and strength that Christ waits to give you. He has been seeking for you. He longs to have you feel your need of his help. He will reach out his hand to grasp the hand stretched out for aid. He declares, "Him that cometh to me I will in no wise cast out." Let mind and heart be enlisted in the warfare against sin. Let your heart soften as you think of how long you have chosen to serve your bitterest foe, while you turned from Him who gave his life for you, who loves you, and who will accept you as his, though you are sinners. Step out from under the rebel flag, and take your stand under the blood-stained banner of Prince Emmanuel.

He who would build up a strong, symmetrical character, must give all and do all for Christ. The Redeemer will not accept divided service. Daily he must learn the meaning of self-surrender. He must study the Word of God, getting its meaning and obeying its precepts. Thus he may reach the highest standard of Christian excellence. There is no limit to the spiritual advancement that he may make if he is a partaker of the divine nature. Day by day God works in him, perfecting the character that is to stand in the day of final test. Each day of his life he ministers to others. The light that is in him shines forth, and stills the strife of tongues. Day by day he is working out before men and angels a vast, sublime experiment, showing what the gospel can do for fallen human beings.

Let us not spare ourselves, but carry forward in earnest the work of reform that must be done in our lives. Let us crucify self. Unholy habits will clamor for the mastery, but in the name and through the power of Jesus we may conquer. To him who daily seeks to keep his heart with all diligence, the promise is given, "Neither death, nor life, nor angels, nor principalities, nor powers, nor things present, nor things to come, nor height, nor depth, nor any other creature, shall be able to separate us from the love of God, which is in Christ Jesus our Lord."

"Thus saith the Lord, the Redeemer of Israel, and his Holy One, to him whom man despiseth, to him whom the nation abhorreth, ... Kings shall see and arise, princes also shall worship, because of the Lord that is faithful, and the Holy One of Israel, and he shall choose thee." God himself is "the justifier of him which believeth in Jesus." And "whom he justified, them he also glorified." Great as is the shame and degradation through sin, even greater will be the honor and exaltation through redeeming love. To human beings, striving for conformity to the divine image, there is imparted an outlay of heaven's treasure, an excellency of power that will place them higher than even the angels who have never fallen.

Also Available By Pastor Bill Liversidge

Victory in Jesus audio series — (5-CD set)

Coming soon:

Victory in Jesus — DVD

The Role and Function of the Holy Spirit — CD Series

The Baptism of the Holy Spirit — CD Series

Our next project:

A God Worthy of Worship — Book

For information and to order, contact Creative Growth Ministries at:

(West Coast)
c/o John Dunbar
916 Cherry Hills Rd.
Bakersfield, CA 93309
661-827-8174
JDUNBAR@back.rr.com

(East Coast)
c/o Joyce Maples
P.O. Box 697
Armuchee, GA 30105
828-403-0653
rejoicing4u@alltel.net

Visit us at our website —www.creativegrowthministries.org — to find more products, audio sermons, and descriptions of some of the seminars offered by Pastor Liversidge.